Farewell Addresses
in
The New Testament

Zacchaeus Studies: New Testament

General Editor: Mary Ann Getty, RSM

Farewell Addresses
in
The New Testament

by

William S. Kurz, S.J.

A Michael Glazier Book
THE LITURGICAL PRESS
Collegeville, Minnesota

About the Author

William S. Kurz, S.J., studied Greek, Latin (M.A.) and Theology (S.T.L.) at St. Louis University; and continued his New Testament studies at Yale University (M.Phil., 1974; Ph.D. 1976). He is on the faculty of Marquette University.

A Michael Glazier Book

published by

THE LITURGICAL PRESS

Cover design by Maureen Daney.
Typography by Brenda Belizzone and Mary Brown.

1   2   3   4   5   6   7   8   9

Library of Congress Cataloging-in-Publication Data

Kurz, William S., 1939-
    Farewell addresses in the New Testament / by William S. Kurz.
        p.   cm. — (Zacchaeus studies. New Testament)
    "A Michael Glazier book."
    Includes bibliographical references (p.) and indexes.
    ISBN 0-8146-5751-6
    1. Farewells in the Bible. 2. Bible. N.T. Acts XX, 17-38-
-Criticism, interpretation, etc. 3. Bible. N.T. Luke XXII, 14-38-
-Criticism, interpretation, etc. 4. Bible. N.T. John XIII-XVII-
-Criticism, interpretation, etc. 5. Narration in the Bible.
    I. Title. II. Series.
    BS2545.F35K87   1990
    226'.06—dc20   90-34560
                                          CIP

Contents

Abbreviations

1 Clem	1 Clement
AB	Anchor Bible
AnBib	Analecta Biblica
BTB	*Biblical Theology Bulletin*
CBQ	*Catholic Biblical Quarterly*
CRINT	Compendia Rerum Iudaicarum ad Novum Testamentum
ExpTim	*Expository Times*
FRLANT	Forschungen zur Religion und Literatur des Alten und Neuen Testaments
HTCNT	Herder's Theological Commentary on the New Testament
HTKNT	Herders theologischer Kommentar zum Neuen Testament
JBL	*Journal of Biblical Literature*
JSNT	*Journal for the Study of the New Testament*
LCL	Loeb Classical Library
LD	Lectio divina
LTP	*Laval théologique et philosophique*
NCB	New Century Bible
NovT	*Novum Testamentum*
NTS	*New Testament Studies*
SANT	Studien zum Alten und Neuen Testament
SBLDS	Society of Biblical Literature Dissertation Series
TCGNT	B. M. Metzger, *A Textual Commentary on the Greek New Testament*
TS	*Theological Studies*

Editor's Note

Zacchaeus Studies provide concise, readable and relatively inexpensive scholarly studies on particular aspects of scripture and theology. The New Testament section of the series presents studies dealing with focal or debated questions; and the volumes focus on specific texts of particular themes of current interest in biblical interpretation. Specialists have their professional journals and other forums where they discuss matters of mutual concern, exchange ideas and further contemporary trends of research; and some of their work on contemporary biblical research is now made accessible for students and others in *Zacchaeus Studies*.

The authors in this series share their own scholarship in non-technical language, in the areas of their expertise and interest. These writers stand with the best in current biblical scholarship in the English-speaking world. Since most of them are teachers, they are accustomed to presenting difficult material in comprehensible form without compromising a high level of critical judgment and analysis.

The works of this series are ecumenical in content and purpose and cross credal boundaries. They are designed to augment formal and informal biblical study and discussion. Hopefully they will also serve as texts to enhance and supplement seminary, university and college classes. The series will also aid Bible study groups, adult education and parish religious education classes to develop intelligent, versatile and challenging programs for those they serve.

Mary Ann Getty
New Testament Editor

Introduction

GOAL OF THIS BOOK

This book will focus especially on three farewells or last testaments in NT narratives, Paul's in Acts 20 and Jesus' in Luke 22 and John 13-17. Since Jesus' eschatological speech in Mark 13 (parallels Lk 21 and Mt 24, with further parables in Mt 25) combines the apocalyptic genre about the endtimes with the farewell, it would take us too far afield. Although 2 Timothy and 2 Peter include much testamental material, their form is that of a farewell letter, not of a farewell speech in a narrative context like Acts 20, Luke 22 and John 13-17. I will address both the farewell address genre with its NT examples and the religious concerns attributed to Jesus and Paul which they contain, such as Church unity, authority as service, correct teaching, the Eucharist, and empowerment by the Holy Spirit. Since I hope to indicate that the farewell genre is especially applicable to the lives of its intended readers and to readers of all generations, I will treat these three farewells not only in their first-century context but also as pertaining to the lives of contemporary Christians, who are the intended readers of this book.

This book is addressed to those who have some familiarity with methods of biblical studies, but it is not written in an overly technical way, so that it can be applicable for university and seminary and adult use. Although I have reflected on the texts in the light of my scholarly training and reading of other critics, the book presents primarily my own position. My hope is that this reflection on the meaning and application of the biblical texts may enrich the lives as well as the minds of believers.

Because my topic is farewell addresses in their narrative

contexts, my analysis will deal with the addresses as a narrative whole, whether or not they are composed of several sources.[1] Because I also am treating the practical concerns of religion and life expressed in these discourses, I will analyse the final canonical form of the three farewell addresses in their biblical contexts, with little attention to the many theories of Johannine sources and redaction. For although scholars have isolated several layers in the Gospel of John and in the farewell address in chapters 13-17, attributing some of this material to sources, some to the evangelist and some to additions by a redactor, their theories will not have much effect on my treatment of the Gospel in its present form.[2] Whether original author or later redactor, whoever was responsible for the current form of John 13-17 was satisfied with these chapters in their present farewell address structure. As I analyse the form and content therefore, my references to the writer or author will relate to whoever was responsible for the extant form of these chapters and will disregard debates about authors and later editors. The same emphasis on the extant form of the document will also apply to the other farewell addresses studied, Luke 22:14-38 and Acts 20:17-38.

My procedure will be to explicate the NT texts with reference to contemporary life. This necessitates multiple methods and approaches: historical critical methods, genre studies, literary narrative criticism, canonical approaches, theological reflection, hermeneutical applications and reflection on the contemporary religious meaning of the biblical texts.[3] The historical critical, form and genre approaches search for the meaning of the text for the original implied readers, to protect against fundamentalist forms of eisegesis and misreading of the text by interpreting it in the wrong context. Before they

---

[1]Cf. M. Sternberg, *The Poetics of Biblical Narrative: Ideological Literature and the Drama of Reading* (Indiana Literary Biblical Series; Bloomington: Indiana University, 1985) 7-23, "Discourse and Source."

[2]E.g., R. Schnackenburg, *The Gospel according to St. John* (3 vols.; HTCNT; New York: Crossroad, 1968-1982) 1.44-74, 3.89-91; R. E. Brown, *The Gospel According to John* (xiii-xxi) (AB 29A; Garden City, NY: Doubleday, 1970) 2.582-94.

[3]For a quick overview of most of these various approaches, see T. Keegan, *Interpreting the Bible: A Popular Introduction to Biblical Hermeneutics* (New York: Paulist, 1985).

apply the text to later concerns, they inquire after its original concerns. The narrative and canonical approaches seek to restore a holistic reading of the narrative text in its biblical and Church contexts after historical criticism has analysed the text into its component parts and separated it from the world of the readers by recalling its historical setting.[4] Finally the theological and hermeneutical approaches go beyond historical and literary description of what the text said to what the statement means and what religious concerns of life it addresses.[5] They attempt to get beyond the mere moving of theological concepts on some ideological chessboard to asking what these concepts mean in human life today.

The recent increase in literary narrative analysis of biblical texts forces some limitation of what I treat—only those concepts and approaches most applicable to the farewell material, especially the *implied reader* and *filling gaps* in the reading process. The recent application to biblical studies of the notion of the *implied reader* offers an important corrective to conjectural reconstructions by historical critics of the communities to whom the text historically was sent.[6] Literary critics have convincingly demonstrated that the text reveals only its implied readers, not whatever real readers happen to pick it up. The implied readers are products of the text itself, the readers as they are imagined and intended by the writer. (I do not have space to discuss the corresponding concept of the implied

[4]Cf. P. Stuhlmacher, *Historical Criticism and Theological Interpretation of Scripture: Toward a Hermeneutics of Consent* (Philadelphia: Fortress, 1977) 90: "It is historically imperative that we resist the hypothetical unravelling of the New Testament tradition into a multiplicity of single strands, solitary communities, and isolated theologies which can no longer be correlated."

[5]Cf. R. E. Brown, *The Critical Meaning of the Bible* (New York: Paulist, 1981) 23-44 and its distinction between "What the Biblical Word Meant and What It Means," though I am not particularly interested in his intramural Catholic polemics.

[6]Cf. W. Kurz, "Narrative Approaches to Luke-Acts," *Biblica* 68 (1987) 195-220, esp. 201 with bibliographical notes; W. Ong, "The Writer's Audience Is Always a Fiction," *Interfaces of the Word: Studies in the Evolution of Consciousness and Culture* (Ithaca: Cornell University, 1977) 53-81; R.A. Fowler, *Loaves and Fishes: The Function of the Feeding Stories in the Gospel of Mark* (SBLDS 54; Chico, CA: Scholars, 1981) ch 4, "Authors and Readers: Reader-Response Criticism and the Gospel of Mark," 149-53, esp. 152, 228 n 16.

author.)[7] As Walter Ong has shown, the writer's audience is *always* a fiction, since the readers are by definition absent as the writers are composing their narratives or even letters.[8] Unlike the oral storyteller who can react and adjust to listeners who are present, the writer has to imagine the readers to whom the narrative is addressed. That imagined reconstruction of the readers by the writer (i.e., the readers "implied" by the writing) may more or less accurately represent the real readers. For example, I may write a letter to a family whom I know imagining them as happy in their situation but unaware of their present grief over the recent diagnosis of cancer in one of their members or of a strain between the parents that has them on the verge of divorce. Similarly, the writer of the Gospel of Luke had an imaginative representation of his intended readers, members of churches that were to use that Gospel. To the extent that the writer knew the actual state and concerns of the members of those churches, to that extent his imagined picture of them would reflect the real readers in those churches. When dealing with ancient texts like the Gospel of Luke or John, critics have only the text itself as evidence for its intended readership. Because we can only ascertain the readers implied by the text and never the real readers, our historical reconstructions are necessarily conjectural. This becomes even more of a problem with an obviously composite document like John's Gospel, with several manifest stages of composition and redaction and correspondingly changing implied readership.[9] Finally, the canonization of narratives like John, Luke and Acts expands the implied readers beyond those originally envisaged by their writers: in canonical criticism, the implied readers of the Christian Bible are all actual and potential Christians of any age, which relativizes even the focus on readers implied by the narrative itself. I intend to

[7]Cf. Kurz, "Narrative Approaches," 206-208 with bibliography; W. Booth, *The Rhetoric of Fiction,* 2nd ed. (Chicago: University of Chicago, 1983) 71-76; Ong, "Audience a Fiction," 57-60.

[8]Ibid.

[9]Cf. R. E. Brown, *The Gospel according to John (i-xii)* (AB 29A; Garden City, NY: Doubleday, 1966) 1.xxiv-xl, and his *The Community of the Beloved Disciple* (New York: Paulist, 1979).

bypass all the hypothetical historical reconstructions of the stages of the Johannine community as I focus first on the narrative concept of the original implied readers of chapters 13-17 in the final composite document, and then on the expanded canonical implied readers of the narratives as part of the biblical canon, especially contemporary Christians.

The second major narrative approach is that of assessing *gaps* which the implied readers are expected to fill during the reading process. Influenced by reader response theories but especially by Meir Sternberg's example of reading gaps in biblical texts, a simplified notion of gaps for our purposes is the "missing links" in the plot or chain of thought, or the matters which the writer does not present and which the reader must provide in order to understand the text.[10]

> From the viewpoint of what is directly given in the language, the literary work consists of bits and fragments to be linked and pieced together in the process of reading: it establishes a system of gaps that must be filled in. This gap-filling ranges from simple linkages of elements, which the reader performs automatically, to intricate networks that are figured out consciously, laboriously, hesitantly, and with constant modifications in the light of additional information disclosed in later stages of the reading.[11]

The process of reading actuates a written text (which, in a sense, is a "dead letter" until it comes to life in the reader's imagination). Narratives which have a structured plot with a beginning, middle and ending differ from purely temporal

---

[10]Sternberg, *Poetics*, ch 6, "Gaps, Ambiguity, and the Reading Process," pp 186-229; W. Iser, "The Reading Process: A Ph omenological Approach," *New Literary History* 3 (1972) 279-99, reprinted in his *The Implied Reader: Patterns in Communication in Prose Fiction from Bunyan to Beckett* (Baltimore: Johns Hopkins, 1974) and in *Reader-Response Criticism: From Formalism to Post-Structuralism*, ed. J. Tompkins (Baltimore: Johns Hopkins, 1980) 274-94; W. Iser, "Interaction between Text and Reader," *The Reader in the Text: Essays on Audience and Interpretation*, ed. S. Suleiman (Princeton, NJ: Princeton Univ., 1980) 106-119; *The Act of Reading: A Theory of Aesthetic Response* (Baltimore: Johns Hopkins Univ., 1978).

[11]Sternberg, *Poetics*, 186.

chronicles ("and then ... and then...") in leaving out un-important steps in the plot, merely suggesting others, and highlighting the most significant. Gaps in the plot which readers are to fill provide interest in the narratives and keep them from being boringly obvious.

Sternberg gives a particularly helpful example of filling gaps with the David and Bathsheba story in 2 Samuel 11.[12] What were David's feelings toward Bathsheba—was he in love or was this a momentary passion (p 197)? Why does the narrator mention Bathsheba's "purifying herself from her uncleanness" right after "and he lay with her" (p 198)? Why does David recall Uriah (the narrator does not tell the readers directly but only through David's actions)? Does Uriah know his wife's infidelity and pregnancy? If not, his answer to David about not going to lie with his wife while his commander is in the fields puts his idealism in ironic contrast to David's behavior. If he does, his answer has a totally different effect: a defiant ironic barb against the king: "I will not 'do this thing' and 'go to my house ... to lie with my wife" (implying "as *you* have done" (p 207). What does David think that Uriah thinks when he sends him back carrying his own death warrant? 1) Uriah does not know about him and Bathsheba? Then he is sending a man of conscience to his death to "save his own skin." 2) Uriah knows? Then why kill him? To marry Bathsheba in any case? 3) David does not know whether Uriah knows? Then his action with Uriah is complex but not very rational, for a conspiracy against Uriah would be obvious if the other soldiers deliberately abandoned him. Therefore (which the readers must supply because the narrator only mentions Joab's action) Joab does not follow David's order exactly, but has many people fall in battle, Uriah among them (pp 209-214). The narrator has only described the bare actions, leaving such questions unanswered and the reader to explain the meaning of the actions.

Like the story of David, the Gospel of John has quite sophis-ticated gaps, which will exercise our ingenuity as readers in trying to fill them and grasp the point of the passage. Why, for

[12]Ibid., 190-222.

instance, does the Gospel wait until the farewell address to mention the "disciple whom Jesus loved," and why does it never name him? Clues from the text guide one in the filling of these gaps and the answering of their questions.

Hermeneutical understanding and application of a text to contemporary concerns is almost always an issue in reading texts, for readers spontaneously question texts from their own perspectives and interests. The greater the distance in time and culture between the perspective of the text and that of the readers, the more necessary becomes a process of hermeneutics to prevent unwarranted identifications between differing cultural values. Farewell addresses lend themselves even more readily to contemporary application than most texts do, because they are intrinsically oriented to the situation after the time of the narrative, and therefore to the implied readers. For since all narratives include a beginning, middle and ending of an event or series of actions,[13] all narratives are past to the time when they are narrated to implied readers. Farewells, which explicitly look ahead beyond the time of the narrative itself, therefore at least implicitly address the time of the implied readers. The farewells in Acts 20, Luke 22 and John 13-17 especially invite questions about their contemporary religious meaning in the lives of their Christian readers. Although the cultural situation of twentieth-century readers differs markedly from that of first century readers implied by the text, the religious meaning of the indwelling Holy Spirit, Church, Eucharist and authority as service applies to all future generations of Christians between Christ's departure to heaven and his return at the end of the world. This is precisely the future religious situation envisaged by the farewell texts. Therefore we can read them (e.g., Christ's prayer "also for those who believe in me through their word" [Jn 17:20]) as addressed to us too.[14]

---

[13]Cf. P. Ricoeur, *Time and Narrative* (3 Vols.; Chicago: Univ. of Chicago, 1984, 1985, 1988) 1.38-42, and Aristotle's *Poetics* (LCL 199; Cambridge, MA: Harvard, 1973).

[14]The mystic Adrienne von Speyr's translated meditations on John 13-17, *John*. vol 3: *The Farewell Discourses* (San Francisco: Ignatius, 1987) also apply the farewell in John to contemporary life.

GENRE OF FAREWELL ADDRESS

The special appeal of farewell addresses is their relationship to the death of a loved one. The last words before the departure of a loved one take on special significance for those remaining behind. Since the moment of death reveals to each person what is ultimately important, and the seemingly important becomes insignificant in the face of death, the last words of those facing death take on special importance for guiding those left behind. These final directives emphasize concerns which in view of their death they considered to be of special moment for future followers.[15] Thus Jesus warns his successors in Luke 22:24-30 not to seek domination over others, but to use the authority that he is giving them to serve the community. In John 13 Jesus gives a final example and exhortation to his disciples to wash each other's feet and thus love one another in humble, serving ways. Final instructions can seal the direction of influence for people's life work among future generations. When Jesus in his farewell address places the twelve apostles as judges of the twelve tribes of the restored Israel (Lk 22:29-30) and gives a special function of authority over the twelve to Peter (Lk 22:32), this is determinative for the authority structure of the community at the beginning of the Acts of the Apostles, where Peter leads the community to restore the twelve by replacing Judas (Acts 1:15-26). Final instructions can revise previous directives, but cannot themselves be further revised except by others. For example, David's farewell address to Solomon in 1 Kings 2:1-9 instructs Solomon to reverse some of David's policies, as in avenging Shimei's curse on David that David had personally sworn not to avenge (vv 8-9). In Luke 22:35-36 Jesus changes his previous directions about setting out on mission "with no purse or bag or sandals" (v 35): "But now, let him who has a purse take it, and likewise

---

[15]Cf. A. B. Kolenkow, "The Literary Genre 'Testament,'" *Early Judaism and Its Modern Interpreters*, ed. R. A. Kraft and G. W. E. Nickelsburg (Philadelphia/Atlanta: Fortress/Scholars, 1986) 259-67, bibliography 279-85, p 259: "Death was believed to be a time when God granted prophetic knowledge and visions of the other world to the righteous. Testaments were viewed as authoritative because no person would be expected to tell an untruth at the hour of death/judgment, nor would the dying person fail to give children both goods and truth (or warning)."

a bag. And let him who has no sword sell his mantle and buy one." The change underscores the new situation of hostility Jesus' followers will face after his death, like the new situation for Shimei after David's death.[16]

Few NT passages so touch Christian hearts and imaginations as deeply as Jesus' farewell in John 13-17, where Jesus loves his own to the end, washes their feet, and instructs them for the time after he leaves this earth for heaven. The washing of the feet has become a prominent part of the Holy Thursday ritual, where Christians re-enact Jesus' powerful symbolic final gesture of loving service as "Teacher and Lord." Christians also instinctively relate to themselves much of what he promises and prophesies in John 13-17. They read as addressed to themselves the promise of the Holy Spirit (Jn 14:16-17, 26; 15:26; 16:7-15), instructions on the vine and branches and communal love (Jn 15:1-17), and Jesus' priestly prayer for his future disciples (Jn 17:20-26). This is not coincidence: the Gospel writer intended John 13-17 to be applied to the readers' lives. He organized this material in the form of a farewell address, namely, Jesus' last words and actions with his disciples before he died. The genre of farewell address gives narrative expression to the special emphasis people pay to the dying requests of those they admire. It portrays the final actions and sayings of a hero like Jesus or Paul or Moses before their death or definitive departure. The farewell setting gives added prominence to the actions and sayings included in it. As in life people recall especially the dying instructions of their parents, so readers tend to remember the dying instructions in a farewell address.

The increased emphasis that comes from inclusion in a farewell address becomes evident from the comparative settings in the synoptic Gospels for the disciples' dispute over who is the greatest. Mark and Matthew include this story on the journey to Jerusalem, after Jesus predicts his passion the third time (Mk 10:35-45, Mt 20:20-28). The readers experience this as just one of many Markan and Matthaean examples of disciples

---

[16]W. Kurz, "Luke 22:14-38 and Greco-Roman and Biblical Farewell Addresses," *JBL* 104 (1985) 251-68, esp. pp 260-61, 266, 268.

not fully understanding Jesus' message. Luke includes it (Lk 22:24-27), without singling out James and John, in Jesus' farewell address at the Last Supper (Lk 22:14-38), not on the way to Jerusalem. The Lukan setting of the dispute about who is the greatest in Jesus' farewell renders it even more shameful. Jesus has just told his disciples that this was his last meal with them. He has just given them the Eucharist. He has just prophesied that one of them would betray him, and they were just questioning one another as to who would do this horrible deed. In these crisis circumstances they begin disputing who among them is to be regarded as greatest! The crisis setting sears Jesus' answer into the readers' memories. They are *not* to be like kings of the Gentiles who lord it over them. Rather, the greatest among them is to become like the youngest, and the leader as one who serves the rest. They are to be like Jesus, who is among them as one who serves them, not lords it over them (Lk 22:24-27). These instructions are among Jesus' last in the narrative. They indicate the concerns most on his mind as he faced his imminent death and separation from his followers.

Final addresses are the last chance in narratives for leaders to provide for the future needs of their organizations and followers. This is the time to name successors and set up institutions that will carry on their work after their departure, if these things have not already been done. This is the time to equip their successors with the powers they need to achieve their mission. Thus Jesus names Peter as the main support for his brothers' faith (Lk 22:31-32) and gives the Eucharist to the Twelve with the command, "Do this in memory of me" (Lk 22:19-20). In John 14-16 Jesus promises the Holy Spirit to his followers to empower their mission of witness and forgiveness of sins and to vindicate Jesus *vis-à-vis* the world's negative judgment on him. Therefore the farewell address is intrinsically oriented to maintaining the traditions and community begun by the founder. Its function for later readers is conservative rather than innovative. Since it concerns those things the dying founders thought of greatest significance for future generations, it implies continuity between the original and later members of their communities. Farewell discourses are the part of a narrative most directly addressed to the implied readers. In Luke, John and Acts for example, Jesus' and Paul's farewell directions for how those who succeeded them are to lead Christians have direct relevance for the lives of later Christian readers.

Farewell addresses were a common genre in the Hellenistic world, and had both Greco-Roman and biblical forms. Testaments were a species of the farewell address genre, which scholars often treat as a synonym.[17] Socrates' farewell in Plato's *Phaedo* inspired many Greco-Roman imitations, but the emphasis in most of those was political or philosphical, often with special focus on how to die nobly. They lacked the emphasis on salvation history and prophecy so central to NT farewells. Actually, most extant Greco-Roman farewells merely ornamented narratives with "last words" in the form of a short witty saying by their heroes. Biblical forms of farewell addresses differed from the Greco-Roman in portraying the speakers more as "men of God" than either as "divine men," as god-men half divine and half human, or in their human nobility.[18] Since the narrative framework of a farewell address is so determinative of the genre, biblical narratives which feature God as the main agent working out his saving plan have their own species of the farewell genre, which differs in tone and worldview from most Greco-Roman narratives in which the hero is the main agent. Not surprisingly the NT farewells have much closer affinities to the earlier biblical examples than to the Greco-Roman forms.[19]

Within this genre of farewell address the form is somewhat elastic. The narrative framework of a farewell address provides its most defining characteristic, that of "a discourse delivered in anticipation of imminent death."[20] Though farewell addresses have many common elements, they do not follow a fixed pattern. They typically feature a father or leader address-

[17]See J. J. Collins, "Testaments," *Jewish Writings of the Second Temple Period,* ed. M. E. Stone (CRINT 2.2; Philadelphia: Fortress, 1984) 325-55, p 325.

[18]Kurz, "Luke 22:14-38," 253-56.

[19]Ibid., 252-53, 257, 267-68, esp. 261.

[20]Collins, "Testaments," 325.

ing his or her sons or successors.[21] Other common elements in biblical farewell addresses include notice of imminent death or final departure, instructions for the time after the speaker's departure, predictions and warnings and ethical exhortations about future problems, transfer of authority, blessings, final prayer and farewell gestures like embraces. For example, the beginning of Jesus' Farewell in John 13-17 provides a notice of his imminent death: "When Jesus knew that his hour had come to depart out of this world to the Father, having loved his own who were in the world, he loved them to the end" (Jn 13:1). Paul predicts his imprisonment and affliction and future trials for the listening elders (his successors as leaders of the Ephesian church):

> And now, behold, I am going to Jerusalem, bound in the Spirit, not knowing what shall befall me there; except that the Holy Spirit testifies to me in every city that imprisonment and afflictions await me.... And now, behold, I know that all you among whom I have gone preaching the kingdom will see my face no more (Acts 20:22-23, 25).

Then he instructs them on how to meet those trials:

> Take heed to yourselves and to all the flock, in which the Holy Spirit has made you overseers, to care for the church of God which he obtained with the blood of his own Son. I know that after my departure fierce wolves will come in among you, not sparing the flock; and from among your own selves will arise men speaking perverse things, to draw away the disciples after them. Therefore, be alert, remembering that for three years I did not cease night or day to admonish every one with tears.... In all these things I have shown you that by so toiling one must help the weak, remembering the words of the Lord Jesus, how he said, "It is more blessed to give than to receive" (Acts 20:28-35).

At the last supper Jesus transfers the authority of the kingdom

---

[21]Ibid., 325-26.

of God to the twelve and places Peter in authority over the others.

> You are those who have continued with me in my trials; and I assign to you, as my Father assigned to me, a kingdom, that you may eat and drink at my table in my kingdom, and sit on thrones judging the twelve tribes of Israel.
> Simon, Simon, behold Satan demanded to have you, that he might sift you like wheat, but I have prayed for you that your faith may not fail; and when you have turned again, strengthen your brethren (Lk 22:28-32).

Moses' farewell in Deuteronomy 31-34 has a whole chapter of blessings of the tribes he was about to leave (Dt 33). At the end of Paul's speech in Acts 20 the narrator describes how Paul prayed with his hearers, and they wept and fell on his neck and kissed him, sorrowing that they would never see his face again (Acts 20:36-38).

The farewell predictions of the departing leader often serve as signposts for future events. If they occur toward the end of a narrative, as in Genesis 49, Deuteronomy 31-33, Acts 20, Luke 22 and John 13-17, they point beyond the time of the narrative to the future time of the readers. If they occur early in a narrative, as in 1 Maccabees 2 and Acts 1:8, they serve as tables of contents for the rest of the narrative. Thus, Mattathias' advice in 1 Maccabees 2:62-63, not to fear the sinner for "his splendor will turn into dung and worms," is fulfilled in the death of the Seleucid tyrant Antiochus IV. His prediction of Judas' military leadership in 2:66, "Judas Maccabeus has been a mighty warrior from his youth; he shall command the army for you and fight the battle against the peoples," is fulfilled in his many victories over the forces of Antiochus. The author describes those victories in language reminiscent of the books of Samuel and Chronicles for the parallel exploits of Saul, Jonathan and especially David, whom Mattathias had singled out for imitation.[22]

Farewells often portray the speaker as a model for disciples'

---

[22]Cf. 1 Macc 2:57; J. Goldstein *I Maccabees* (AB 41; Garden City, NY: Doubleday, 1976) 242, 248, 342.

behavior, as Jesus is in washing their feet (Jn 13) or Paul is in faithfully teaching the whole gospel and working for his own support (Acts 20). Living models of behavior are important for the exhortatory and educational intent of ancient and biblical farewell speeches. Ethical and religious teachers were expected to illustrate their teaching by their behavior, just as a contemporary coach or director teaches fundamentals to the team or cast not only by words but by demonstrating them in action. In the ancient world students usually had only a single teacher or master. Students not only listened to the masters' teachings but apprenticed themselves to them, often living with them and observing the model they provided of daily living as well as of the trade, art or philosophy being learned.[23] The last teaching before the teacher's death or departure included both verbal instructions and the example of the teacher's actions in the light of that death or departure. Socrates in Plato's *Phaedo* not only gave his disciples his final teachings on the meaning of death, but pointed to his lack of sorrow and fear before his death as the most persuasive aspect of his teaching on death. So Jesus' example of self-effacing love for his disciples when he washed their feet underlined his verbal teaching on loving and serving one another in John 13.

The main purpose of biblical farewell addresses was to provide narrative transition and continuity between founders or heroes and their successors and later generations of followers or descendants. They also called later generations back to traditional concerns. Because they were specifically addressed to the generations after those featured in the narrative, they had a special relationship to the readers implied by the narrative, and they could often be read as directly addressed to them. Farewell addresses have more contemporary relevance than most parts of a narrative, which by definition concerns the past.[24] An example of a farewell discourse that addresses

---

[23]See W. Kurz, "Kenotic Imitation of Paul and of Christ in Philippians 2 and 3," *Discipleship in the New Testament*, ed. F. Segovia (Philadelphia: Fortress, 1985) 103-126, esp. pp 106-109; B. Fiore, *The Function of Personal Example in the Socratic and Pastoral Epistles* (AnBib 105; Rome: Biblical Institute, 1986).

[24]Cf. Aristotle's classic definition in his *Poetics* that a narrative has a beginning, middle and ending; the fact that it has an end implies that it must have taken place in the past.

the readers of the work as much as the listeners in the narrative is Jesus' prayer for "those who believe in me through their word" (Jn 17:20), i.e., Christian readers. Farewell addresses often refer beyond the time of the narrative into the future time of the readers envisaged by the author, as when Jesus promises in John's Gospel that "they will put you out of synagogues" (Jn 16:2), and Paul warns in Acts that "after my departure fierce wolves will come in among you . . . and from among your own selves will arise men speaking perverse things. . . ." (Acts 20:29-30). The intended readers of John most probably experienced or knew of expulsion from synagogues, and the readers of Acts probably experienced false teachings both from wandering teachers and from leaders of their own communities.

Prophecies by an illustrious ancestor, founder or past leader, which play such a central role in farewell addresses, interpret the time of the readers as foretold by God and therefore part of his plan. Distressing incidents in the lives of the readers become more understandable when seen as part of God's plan from of old. They are not meaningless afflictions but foreseen by God who remains in control of history, even when he seems to be absent in such tribulations. The readers' sufferings become more bearable when understood as foreseen and forewarned. In this sense the testament can be described as "a genre of difficult times," that "allows the present generation to relate itself both to present difficulty and the relevance of God to that present."[25] The fact that God predicted in the past that the present generation would suffer persecution and false teachers assures those who are suffering that God has not forgotten them and will provide for them in their distress. False teachers do not mean that God has abandoned his Church; he warned future generations to be ready for them. Persecutions do not necessarily mean that the present Church has done something wrong, since past disciples were forewarned about them.

Promises and prophecies from farewell addresses also legiti-

---

[25]Kolenkow, "Genre 'Testament,'" 263, citing H. J. Michel, *Die Abschiedsrede des Paulus an die Kirche Apg 20 17-38* (SANT 35; Munich: Ksel, 1973).

mize current offices and structures which they have foretold.
Jacob's farewell blessing of Judah in Genesis 49:8-12 legitimizes the Davidic line from Judah as lasting ruler of the
twelve tribes.

> The scepter shall not depart from Judah, nor the ruler's
> staff from between his feet, until he comes to whom it
> belongs, and to him shall be the obedience of the peoples
> (Gen 49:10).

Mattathias' reference in 1 Maccabees 2:54 to "the covenant of
everlasting priesthood" of "Phinehas our father" legitimizes
the priestly role of the Maccabean dynasty. In light of this, his
last charge to his sons sanctions the civil and priestly leadership
of Simeon and the military headship of Judas.

> Now behold, I know that Simeon your brother is wise in
> counsel; always listen to him; he shall be your father. Judas
> Maccabeus has been a mighty warrior from his youth; he
> shall command the army for you and fight the battle against
> the peoples (1 Macc 2:65-66).

Jesus' special mission to Peter in Luke 22:31-32 legitimizes his
leadership among the twelve.

> Simon, Simon, behold, Satan demanded to have you, that
> he might sift you like wheat, but I have prayed for you that
> your faith may not fail; and when you have turned again,
> strengthen your brethren (Lk 22:31-32).

The Greek OT had several farewell addresses that provided
examples of these elements for the Evangelists. The classic
farewell passages were Jacob's farewell to his sons, the patriarchs of Israel's twelve tribes, in Genesis 49, and Moses' farewell in Deuteronomy 31-33, which later farewell addresses in
the biblical tradition imitated. To understand the basic form
of the farewell address it is easier to begin with the later more
stereotyped examples before looking at Genesis 49 and
Deuteronomy 31-33, for although the Genesis and Deuteronomy examples provided the inspiration for most of the other

biblical instances, their later, shorter imitations are clearer examples of the farewell form. Many of the individual pro- phecies in Genesis 49 are too poetic to be clear, and some of its negative predictions, like the rejection of Simeon and Levi, were an embarrassment for later writings because of the impor- tance of the Levitical priesthood. Deuteronomy 31-33 is too long and its material is too diverse to provide a sharp paradigm of a farewell address. Much clearer examples of the farewell form are the later farewell addresses modeled on these arche- typal ones, which became more stereotyped through imitation, such as the two versions of the farewell of Mattathias, father of the Maccabees, in 1 Maccabees 2:49-70 and Josephus, *Jewish Antiquities* 12.6.3, 279-84. Comparing these two ver- sions can illustrate both some of the constant elements in the genre and how variations are related to differences in implied readers. For Josephus rewrites for a broader Greco-Roman audience the biblical version of 1 Maccabees that was intended for Hellenized Jews, in language that would be meaningful also to Hellenistic non-Jews unfamiliar with the biblical tra- dition. This comparison therefore exemplifies both major types of ancient farewell addresses found during the Hellenistic age in which the NT was written.

1 Maccabees begins with a notice that Mattathias was about to die and spoke to his sons.

> Arrogance and reproach have now become strong; it is a time of ruin and furious anger. Now, my children, show zeal for the law [singular, *nomos*], and give your lives for the covenant of our fathers (1 Macc 2:49b-50).

Josephus adds more explicit farewell aspects in his Greco- Roman rewriting of the scene:

> But after being in command for a year, he fell ill, and calling his sons, made them stand around him, and said, "I myself, my sons, am about to go the destined [*hei- marmenēn*] way, but my spirit [*phronēma*] I leave in your keeping, and I beg you not to be unworthy guardians of it, but to be mindful of the purpose of him who begot you and brought you up, and to preserve our country's customs and

> to restore our ancient form of government [*archaian politeian*], which is in danger of passing away, and not to make common cause with those who are betraying it whether of their own will or through compulsion; but since you are my sons, I wish you to remain constant as such and to be superior to all force and compulsion, being so prepared in spirit as to die for the laws [plural, vs. the biblical singular *nomos*], if need be, and bearing this in mind, that when the Deity [*to theion*] sees you so disposed, He will not forget you, but in admiration of your heroism [*aretēs*] will give [sic] back to you again, and will restore to you your liberty, in which you shall live securely and in the enjoyment of your own customs (*Ant.* 12, 6, 3, 279-81 LCL 7, p. 145).

Josephus uses the pagan term *destined* or *fated* way rather than biblical expressions of God's providence or phrases like "join my fathers." The word for *spirit* is not the word used in the Greek OT and NT for a personal spirit (*pneuma*), but an abstract noun that connotes high spirit, resolution, pride.[26] Instead of the normal biblical names for God Josephus refers abstractly to "the Deity," and he uses an expression for heroism which is more common in non-biblical Hellenism than in the Bible. Whereas Mattathias in 1 Maccabees refers in a biblical manner to the "deeds of the fathers" (2:51a) such as the tests of Abraham and Joseph, the zeal and everlasting priesthood of "Phinehas our father" (2:54), and the deeds of Joshua, Caleb, David and others (2:51-60), in Josephus he recalls instead his own example and purpose in bringing up his sons and replaces the biblical comparison to the fathers' deeds with the Hellenistic concerns of preserving "our country's customs" and restoring "our ancient form of government" (280, p 145). Whereas 1 Maccabees has the Hellenistic Jewish exhortation, "My children, be courageous [*andrizesthe*] and grow strong in the law [singular], for by it you will gain honor [or "be glori-

---

26"*phronēma,*" *A Greek-English Lexicon,* H. G. Liddell, R. Scott, H. S. Jones (Oxford: Clarendon, 1968) p. 1956.

fied," *doxasthēsesthe*]" (2:64),[26a] Josephus replaces the biblical singular term, *law*, with the neutral plural *laws*, and rewrites the biblical "be glorified" (as in John's Gospel) with a more pagan or philosophical emphasis on being in love with immortality (vs. being in love with God in Scripture) through glory (in the sense of good reputation) and the memory of one's deeds:

> For though our bodies are mortal and subject to death, we can, through the memory of our deeds, attain the heights of immortality; it is this which I wish you to be in love with, and for its sake to pursue glory [or "good repute," *eukleian*] and undertake the greatest tasks and not shrink from giving up your lives for them (282, p 145).

To the Maccabean naming of Simeon and Judas as authorities over the others, Josephus adds an emphasis on unity, "Most of all I urge you to be of one mind [*homonoein*]" (283 p 145), as well as a non-biblical Hellenistic reference to talents [*aretaí*]. Both versions share the following further embodiments of farewell genre elements: commissioning the sons to rally others and avenge wrongs, Mattathias' prayer or blessing, his death and burial and the people's mourning for him, and Judas Maccabaeus' replacing him as head of the army (1 Macc 2:67-70, *Antiquities* 12, 6, 3-4, 284-85). The two versions thus illustrate both some constant elements of the genre and how differences between them relate to the different implied readers.

In light of these constant elements as illustrated by the Maccabean and Josephus versions of Mattathias' farewell address, let us look at the classic biblical examples of Genesis 49 and Deuteronomy 31-34.

GENESIS 49: Jacob's testament to the heads of the twelve tribes in Genesis 49 was perhaps the archetypal testament for   – ✓

[26a]"Since 1 Maccabees also stems from the time of the Hellenistic empires after Alexander the Great and interacts with that environment, its intended Jewish readers are also to some extent Hellenized, so that both 1 Macc and Josephus have Hellenistic elements. Cf. the correction of the dichotomy between Hellenism and Judaism in M. Hengel, *Judaism and Hellenism* (2 vols; Philadelphia: Fortress, 1974) esp. pp 310-14.

the later biblical tradition. Several intertestamental farewell addresses imitate it also, not only the *Testaments of the Twelve Patriarchs*, but *Jubilees* 21 (Abraham), 36 (Isaac), and 35:18-20, 27 (Rebecca).

   The testament begins with Jacob calling his sons: "Gather yourselves together, that I may tell you what shall befall you in the days to come" (Gen 49:1). The stage is set for blessings (or curses, as appropriate) that foreshadow the destinies of the twelve tribes. Reuben the first born is cursed and removed from his pre-eminence because he defiled his father's bed (vv 3-4); the tribe of Reuben is later overcome by the Moabites (Jg 5:15-16, Dt 33:6). Simeon and Levi are rejected for their violence against Shechem which got Jacob in trouble with the Canaanites (Gen 34:25-30); Simeon is eventually absorbed into Judah, and Levi reduced from a full tribe to a priestly class (Ex 32:26-29). Judah receives the blessing of the scepter and pre-eminence over the other tribes. "Judah, your brothers shall praise you . . . your father's sons shall bow down before you. Judah is a lion's whelp. . . . The scepter shall not depart from Judah, nor the ruler's staff from between his feet, until he comes to whom it belongs, and to him shall be the obedience of the peoples. . . ." (vv 8-10). The oracle is fulfilled in David, perhaps further elaborated in later oracles like Isaiah 11:1-9, and becomes a source of messianic expectations for the NT. Other oracles predict that Zebulun shall get access to the Mediterranean (from Asher's territory), Issachar will become subservient to the Canaanites, Dan will get full tribal prestige through guerrilla warfare, Gad will bravely repel Ammonite marauders (Jg 11), Asher will have very rich land, and Naphtali will experience freedom and vitality (vv 13-21). However, many of these predictions are so obscurely described in poetic metaphors as to be opaque. Jacob's blessing predicts that the tribe of Joseph (treated as a unity before being divided into the tribes of Ephraim and Manasseh, as in Moses' farewell, Dt 33:13-17) shall be populous and mighty in war and blessed by God (vv 22-26). The blessing for Benjamin refers to warlike attributes (v 27). After blessing the twelve tribes, Jacob predicts his imminent death and charges his sons to bury him with his ancestors in the cave Abraham bought as a grave site (vv 29-32). The testament ends with his death: "When Jacob finished charging his sons, he drew up his feet into the bed, and breathed his last, and was gathered to his people" (v 33).

DEUTERONOMY 31-34: The farewell words and death of Moses in Deuteronomy 31-34 were also a favorite prototype for later testaments such as the *Testament of Moses,* Pseudo-Philo's *Biblical Antiquities* 19 and Josephus' *Jewish Antiquities* 4.8.45-49, 309-31. These chapters are not a unified farewell address, however. They gather material from the book's narrator (cc 31, 32:44-33:1, and 34) and the pre-existing Song of Moses (Dt 32) and blessing of Moses (Dt 33). Many of the farewell elements come in the words of the Lord to Moses (e.g., Dt 31:14, 16-21) rather than from Moses to Joshua or the Israelites, though those also are present (e.g., Dt 31:2-6, 7-8, 10-13, 26-29, plus the Song and blessing of Moses in Dt 32 and 33). Chapters 31-34 of Deuteronomy more clearly exemplify components of farewell situations than the form of a unified farewell address.

Deuteronomy 31 begins the final farewell section of the book with Moses referring to his departure:

> I am a hundred and twenty years old this day; I am no longer able to go out and come in. The Lord has said to me, "You shall not go over this Jordan" (Dt 31:2).

Moses promises that God will be present with the Israelites to enable them to conquer the land, so he encourages them not to fear (31:6). He summons his successor Joshua, exhorts him before the people to lead them with courage into the land (31:7) for the Lord will go before them (31:8), and legislates a covenant ceremony of rededication to the law (31:9-13). Then the Lord commissions Joshua as Moses' successor (31:14-23):

> And the Lord said to Moses, "Behold, the days approach when you must die; call Joshua, and present yourselves in the tent of meeting, that I may commission him." And Moses and Joshua went and presented themselves in the tent of meeting... [vv 14-15]. And the Lord said to Moses, "Behold, you are about to sleep with your fathers; then this people will rise and play the harlot after the strange gods of the land, where they go to be among them, and they will

forsake me and break my covenant which I have made with
them. Then my anger will be kindled against them ... and
many evils and troubles will come upon them, so that they
will say in that day, 'Have not these evils come upon us
because our God is not among us?' ... [vv 16-17]. Now
therefore write this song, and teach it to the people of
Israel... [v 19]. And when many evils and troubles have
come upon them, this song shall confront them as a
witness..." [v 21]. So Moses wrote this song the same day,
and taught it to the people of Israel.

And the Lord commissioned Joshua the son of Nun and
said, "Be strong and of good courage; for you shall bring
the children of Israel into the land which I swore to give
them: I will be with you" (Dt 31:14-17, 19, 21-23).

This section illustrates several important elements of farewells—
prediction of imminent death, commission of a successor,
prophecy of coming defection and punishment, and promise
of help in the commissioned task—but in the form of speeches
by the Lord rather than a farewell speech by Moses.

After Moses had the law book placed in the ark as a witness
against future rebellion after his death, he had the Levites
assemble the leaders for a farewell warning against future
apostasy (Dt 31:24-29). "Then Moses spoke the words of this
song until they were finished, in the ears of all the assembly of
Israel" (Dt 31:30). After incorporating the Song of Moses, an
old independent psalm about the history of the relationship
between God and Israel, in chapter 32:1-43, Deuteronomy
returned to its farewell framework, stating that Moses and
Joshua recited the song before the people (Dt 32:44). Moses
spoke further:

Lay to heart all the words which I enjoin upon you this day,
that you may command them to your children, that they
may be careful to do all the words of this law. For it is no
trifle for you, but it is your life, and thereby you shall live
long in the land which you are going over the Jordan to
possess (Dt 32:46-47).

Such warnings against future apostasy became very important in the biblical farewell tradition, as in Acts 20. In Deuteronomy the Lord then told Moses he will die on Mount Nebo after seeing but not entering the promised land (Dt 32:48-52).

Another independent poem, Moses' blessing of the twelve tribes, follows in Deuteronomy 33, which is similar in structure to Jacob's blessing of the twelve patriarchs in Genesis 49. After a recapitulation of how God saved Israel and gave them the law (Dt 33:2-5), Moses blesses each of the tribes. The content of these blessings often differs markedly from the blessings of Jacob, reflecting the changed circumstances of the tribes between the time of the writing of Genesis 49 and Deuteronomy 33 (and thus, to some extent, differences in the situations of the implied readers). Rather than Jacob's curse on Simeon and Levi (Gen 49:5-7), for example, Moses gives Levi a special blessing with the prerogatives of the priesthood (Dt 33:8-11), which reflects the importance of the Levitic priests in later Israel. Judah, on the other hand, no longer has the messianic prominence of Gen 49:8-12 ("the scepter shall not depart from Judah..."), but needs help from the other tribes (Dt 33:7). When these blessings were composed, Joseph's prestige seems greater than Judah's: "Let these come upon the head of Joseph, and upon the crown of the head of him that is prince among his brothers" (Dt 33:16). The poem of Moses' blessings ends with praise to the God of Israel, who rescued them and will protect them (Dt 33:26-29).

Deuteronomy 34 finishes the narrative framework after all the farewell speeches and blessings. Many of the details are standard descriptions of the situation after a farewell speech: the hero's death and burial and mourning (34:1-8), the passing of the person's "spirit" and authority to the successor (v 9), and praise of the hero (vv 10-12).

The biblical and extrabiblical examples of Genesis 49, Deuteronomy 31-34, 1 Maccabees 2:47-70 and Josephus, *Jewish Antiquities* 12.6.3, 279-84 illustrate both the basic genre of farewell address and the wide variety of actual speeches. Other examples from the OT milieu could be added, such as Samuel's farewell to the Israelites in 1 Samuel 12, David's to Solomon in 1 Kings 2:1-10, Joshua's in Joshua 23-24, the *Testaments of the Twelve Patriarchs*, the *Testament of Moses*, and Jacob's farewell in *Jubilees* 22:10-30.[27] But enough examples have been shown to illustrate the basic form of the genre, which portrays leaders saying farewell to their successors or the people and preparing them for the time after their deaths.

A summary of the main elements of OT farewell addresses can help recall the contours of the form before analyzing the NT farewell addresses in Acts 20, Luke 22 and John 13-17. Most OT farewell discourses begin with a notice of the speaker's impending death and a summoning of his or her successors. They include many of the following elements: prophecies and warnings about the future, especially future apostasy; God's promises for the future; exhortation to the successors to do and pass on these instructions; reference to the "deeds of the fathers" as models; naming authorities and commissioning them for future tasks; prayers and blessings (or curses); notice of the speaker's death and burial and the people's mourning; succession in authority; and praise of the speaker. Many of these elements appear in the NT farewell addresses in Acts 20, Luke 22 and John 13-17.

[27]See Kurz, "Luke 22:14-38."

1

Acts 20

INTRODUCTION

Paul's farewell to the Ephesian elders in Acts 20 is the most straightforward and clearest example of a farewell address in the New Testament. Because there is nothing in Acts 20 to distract from its being a farewell speech, it is a good place to begin treatment of that genre.[28] John 13-17, with its many strands and repetitions, which probably stem from multiple sources, obscures the structure of the farewell form. Luke 22:14-38 is composed of many traditions, which have drawn attention to themselves and away from the farewell context into which Luke has placed them.

The introductory chapter showed the flexibility of the genre of farewell address, how it has elements common to most but not to all such speeches. The farewell speech in Acts 20 exhibits the following elements, all of which are commonly found in the genre, especially in its biblical variety: (1) summoning of successors; (2) the speaker as model for imitation; (3) allusion to imminent death; (4) apologetic for the conduct of one's office; (5) warnings about future false teachers; (6) exhortation to faithful leadership; (7) blessings; (8) prayers together; (9) farewell gestures.

Acts 20 contextualizes these common elements into the fol-

---

[28]Many have treated Acts 20:17-38 as a farewell speech: see the recent treatments and bibliographical guides to the earlier literature in G. Schneider, *Die Apostelgeschichte: II. Teil* (HTKNT 5.2; Freiburg: Herder, 1982) 290-300; P.-R. Tragan, "Les 'destinataires' du discours de Milet: Une approche du cadre communautaire d'Ac 20,18-35," *A cause de l'évangile: Études sur les Synoptiques et les Actes offertes au P. Jacques Dupont, O.S.B. à l'occasion de son 70e anniversaire* (LD 123; Paris: Cerf, 1985) 779-98; J. Lambrecht, "Paul's Farewell-Address at Miletus (Acts 20,17-38)," *Les Actes des Apôtres: Traditions, rédaction, théologie*, ed. J. Kremer (Leuven-Gembloux: University-J. Duculot, S.A., 1979) 307-37; Kurz, "Luke 22:14-38," 252.

lowing structural elements of Paul's farewell address to the Ephesian elders: (1) Paul summons the elders who are responsible for the church after his departure for a final discourse. (2) He points to himself as a model for them to follow. (3) By stating they will never see him again, he clearly alludes to his coming death. (4) He declares he has not failed in his obligations to the people. (5) He foretells problems like apostasy and false teachers after his departure. (6) He exhorts them to oversee the church faithfully. (7) He commends the elders to God, (8) prays with them, and (9) exchanges farewell gestures with them.

The speech itself signals its main subdivisions by the phrases "And now, behold" (vv 22, 25) and "And now" (v 32). Therefore my analysis will follow the order and divisions of the speech, relating each to the common elements listed above.

The narrator introduces the speech in Acts 20:17-18: "And from Miletus he sent to Ephesus and called to him the elders of the church. And when they came to him, he said to them: ..." This introduction is the first farewell element, Paul's summoning of the elders who are responsible for the church after his departure for a final discourse.

Paul (the speaker), the Ephesian elders (the audience), and the farewell address itself make up the three ordinary elements of the rhetorical situation in Acts 20. In the Acts of the Apostles, the speaker Paul is featured more than any other Christian missionary or apostle, for he is the most important witness to God's word after Jesus himself. Therefore Acts gives special attention to his farewell speech. The narrator first introduces Paul ("a young man named Saul") at the stoning of Stephen (Acts 7:58-8:1) and as persecuting the Church (Acts 8:3). In chapter 9, the narrator describes Saul's transformation from persecutor to champion of the faith. Paul retells the same incident twice in speeches at his trials in Acts 22 and 26. The threefold repetition of this event is a Lukan pattern of emphasis (as in the three accounts of the conversion of Cornelius' household [Acts 10-11 and 15] and of the "apostolic decree" enabling Gentile and Jewish Christian table fellowship [Acts 15:20, 29; 21:25]). Paul's change from persecutor to preacher of the faith is one of the most important examples in Luke-Acts of how God reverses human fortunes and values.

More than half of the Acts (chaps 13-28) describes the missionary journeys and the trials of Paul, the book's main hero and the apostolic figure best known to the author. Through his preaching and healings, Paul spreads the word of God and founds churches through much of Asia, Macedonia and Greece. As in the beginning of Acts Peter spreads Christianity throughout Jerusalem and Judea, so Paul spreads it through Asia and into Europe. From Acts 21-28, Paul undergoes trials parallel to those of Jesus in Luke 22-23.[29] Thus the Lukan narrator has portrayed Paul in roles parallel to those of Jesus and Peter. After Jesus himself, Peter and Paul provide the foundations of the Church in Acts.

The narrator says no more about Peter after mentioning him at the "Council of Jerusalem" in Acts 15. The only two heroes whose deaths he treats in detail are Jesus and Paul. Only Jesus and Paul have farewell addresses in Luke-Acts (Lk 22:14-38, Acts 20:17-38). Though the narrator mentions Peter's early imprisonments, he is silent about those leading to Peter's later death, but emphasizes the trials leading to Jesus' and Paul's deaths.[30] Thus, the Paul who gives his farewell address in Acts 20 is for Acts the most important witness to God's word after Jesus himself. As such, his final words merit special attention.

The elders of the church at Ephesus provide the audience for the Acts 20 speech. Though the narrator refers to more than two years of Paul's missionary activity in Ephesus (Acts 19:8-10) and incidents like the Jewish exorcists (19:11-19) and the silversmith riot (19:23-41), he does not mention the elders of the church at Ephesus until he introduces Paul's farewell to them (20:17). All we know of them is mentioned in this speech, that they are now responsible for overseeing the church at Ephesus after Paul's departure. They do not even

[29]E.g. both Jesus and Paul appear before Roman Procurators with Jewish accusers, both appear before a Herodian, the procurator declares both are innocent but they are not freed in Lk 23:1-25 and Acts 25-26. See R. F. O'Toole, *The Unity of Luke's Theology: An Analysis of Luke-Acts* (Good News Studies, 9; Wilmington: Michael Glazier, 1984) 67-73.

[30]Of course Paul's death is only prophesied, not reported, in Acts itself (see Acts 20:23, 25, 38).

meet Paul at Ephesus, but Paul calls them instead to nearby Miletus because he was bypassing Ephesus in the haste of his return to Jerusalem. The implied readers know about Christian elders, both from their own church experience and from earlier treatment of elders in Acts. Especially important is Acts 14:23, which describes how Paul and Barnabas placed elders over all of the churches they founded. "And when they had appointed elders for them in every church, with prayer and fasting they committed them to the Lord in whom they believed" (Acts 14:23). Christian elders are also mentioned in Judea (Acts 11:30) and with the apostles in Jerusalem (Acts 15:2, 4, 6, 22-23). In Acts 11:29-30, Christians from Antioch determined to send famine relief to Christians in Judea, "and they did so, sending it to the elders by the hand of Barnabas and Saul" (11:30). In Acts 15, the rulers of the Jerusalem church are the apostles and elders: "Paul and Barnabas and some of the others were appointed to go up to Jerusalem to the apostles and elders about this question" (Acts 15:2) concerning circumcision of gentile Christians. The Ephesian elders' weeping and farewell kisses at the end of Paul's speech illustrate their love for Paul. The audience in Acts 20 are unnamed church leaders, probably appointed by Paul (as in Acts 14:23), who love Paul and are now responsible for protecting and promoting the gospel Paul preached.

The first section of Paul's speech follows in Acts 20:19-21:

> You yourselves know how I lived among you all the time from the first day that I set foot in Asia, serving the Lord with all humility and with tears and with trials which befell me through the plots of the Jews; how I did not shrink from declaring to you anything that was profitable, and teaching you in public and from house to house, testifying both to Jews and to Greeks of repentance to God and of faith in our Lord Jesus Christ.

Paul's speech thus begins with the second farewell element, presenting himself as a model for the elders to follow. His own ministry exemplifies total dedication to preaching the entire gospel message. This speech will also end with the same farewell element of using himself as a model for the elders to imitate. Thus, in Acts 20:33-35, Paul points to his example of supporting his own ministry (with its implied motive of not distracting from his preaching of the gospel by appealing for money):

> I coveted no one's silver or gold or apparel. You yourselves know that these hands ministered to my necessities, and to those who were with me. In all things I have shown you that by so toiling one must help the weak, remembering the words of the Lord Jesus, how he said, 'It is more blessed to give than to receive.'

It was not ostentatious or egotistic for Paul to point to himself as a model for his successors to follow. This was an expected element in farewell discourses. His culture highly esteemed the importance of living examples of behavior, whether of ruling, of virtuous living, or even of doing philosophy.[31] Teaching was quite different from contemporary formats in which students take four or more lecture courses by different teachers each semester, so that they may have up to forty teachers in college. Hence teachers as we know them do not act so clearly as singular role models. At the time of the NT, teaching involved a much more evident apprenticeship under a master. Disciples not only listened to formal teachings but imitated the teacher as he or she lived these truths in his or her life. Thus when Paul called the Ephesian elders to imitate both his manner of pastoring the church and of living his Christian life, he was only doing what was expected of him.

The role of example is an important and often overlooked element of Christian church leadership. Preaching without a corresponding exemplary life can become totally discredited. Paul's example of supporting himself and his co-workers with the work of his own hands was a strong protection against the scandal of preachers amassing wealth they beg from the poor. Paul pointed to how he lived his life of ministry while he was among the Ephesians. He "slaved for" the Lord in all humility and at great personal cost amidst persecutions.

By pointing to his own precedent, Paul provides a prototype of a Christian minister of the gospel that is meant to be

---

[31]See Fiore, *Personal Example.*

imitated by Christian pastors of all ages. For example, like Paul, preachers should not be afraid to proclaim and teach whatever is necessary for their hearers' salvation, no matter how unpleasant that message might be (Acts 20:20-21). Thus Paul sets an example of preaching repentance to God (Acts 20:21). Repentance implies that those repenting are in the wrong, which is not what most congregations are itching to hear (cf. 2 Tim 4:3). Preaching repentance, so central to all NT preaching, cannot be done without straightforward teaching about what is sinful and what is not. That is why NT exhortation so often includes representative lists of sinful behaviors. Galatians has a well-known example:

> Now the works of the flesh are plain: immorality, impurity, licentiousness, idolatry, sorcery, enmity, strife, jealousy, anger, selfishness, dissension, party spirit, envy, drunkenness, carousing, and the like. I warn you, as I warned you before, that those who do such things shall not inherit the kingdom of God (Gal 5:19-21).

Such direct preaching of sin and repentance is not nearly as much in evidence in many contemporary sermons.

The biblical emphasis on repentance, mentioned again in Acts 20, seems strange to modern ears. What does it mean, and why is it so central in biblical preaching in both the OT and NT?

The call to repentance makes sense only in view of the biblical perspective on sin. Though there are many biblical theologies, one can take a canonical approach to a topic like sin, for a unified thread runs through the canonical discussions of sin. The canonical treatment of sin begins with the fall of Adam and Eve in Genesis 3. Its alienating and destructive effects proliferate in the rest of the primeval history of Genesis 4-11.

Genesis 1-3 teaches that God created the human race in his image to be his stewards over the rest of creation. He created humans exalted, but they tried to exalt themselves even more to "be like God" (Gen 3:5). God created humans good, not evil (Gen 1:31), but they chose to reject God's commandment and thus became oriented to evil. God created male and female to be two in one and totally naked before each other without shame (Gen 2:24-25), but when they sinned against God they became ashamed of their nakedness and "covered up" from each other (3:7).[32] When they refused to accept personal responsibility for their sin but blamed another (3:12-13), they destroyed the unity in which God created them and have since been alienated from each other (3:16-17a). Since their sin, they and their descendants, the whole human race, live as fallen from God's grace and as alienated from God and one another (esp. 3:23-24 and 4:5-10, Cain's murder of Abel). Their fallenness inclines them more to self-centeredness and evil than to generosity, goodness and obedience to their Creator. All humans are born into this situation of fallenness and alienation and all need to be saved from it and from their own sins:

> all, both Jews and Greeks, are under the power of sin, as it is written: "None is righteous, no, not one; no one understands, no one seeks for God. All have turned aside, together they have gone wrong; no one does good, not even one" (Rom 3:9-12).

This situation underlies the NT preaching of repentance. Sin is rejection of God and God's authority as Creator over oneself. Sin is primarily a personal affront against God by rejecting his commands, not the legalistic breaking of some impersonal law. In the popular though usually subconscious game of legalism, where one tries to break or stretch the written law as much as possible without penalty, broken positive laws do not necessarily demand repentance. But broken laws that also fracture one's relationship with the lawgiver do require repentance. "Have you eaten of the tree of which I commanded you not to eat?" (Gen 3:11). Direct disobedience to their Creator challenged his authority and insulted him personally, thus alienating humans from God.

---

[32]W. Kurz, "Genesis and Abortion: An Exegetical Test of a Biblical Warrant in Ethics," *TS* 47 (1986) 668-80, esp. pp 672-73: though scholars have isolated two sources in Genesis 1-3, they can and must be interpreted canonically as mutually interpretative. See B. S. Childs, *Introduction to the Old Testament as Scripture* (Philadelphia: Fortress, 1979) 149-50.

Repentance involves admission that one has done wrong, regret for the wrong done (especially for rejecting God or his commands), renunciation of the wrong, and some intention to try to avoid that kind of wrongdoing in the future. There is no repentance without admitting one's sin. Nor can those who refuse to admit their wrongdoing receive the forgiveness of another, even of God. From the viewpoint of the people offended, refusal by the offenders to admit being wrong is most frustrating. When loved ones hurt them and they desire to forgive them and restore their relationship, they experience deep helplessness when the offenders refuse to admit their guilt. If someone says "I forgive you for X," and the other says, "I did nothing wrong," or "X was *your* fault," the latter has not accepted the first's forgiveness. The act of forgiveness is aborted because it cannot be implanted in the recipient.

The general biblical teaching is that all humans have sinned against God. Therefore all need to repent to God who desires to forgive them and reconcile them to himself. The general NT teaching is that God has reconciled the world to himself by sending his Son to atone for its sins. Jesus' obedience unto his own undeserved death restores the relationship broken by Adam's disobedience leading to his deserved death. To participate in this reconciliation with God, sinful humans have to repent of their sins, believe in Jesus as their savior who reconciles them to God, and allow him to do so. This is why repentance plays such a critical role in NT preaching, and why Christian evangelists asked their listeners to "repent and believe the good news" (Jesus as reported in Mk 1:15).

As its model of a Christian minister, Paul is also portrayed in Acts 20 as typifying the necessity to preach "faith in our Lord Jesus Christ" (v 21). NT preaching concentrates on Jesus Christ, not on issues. Salvation comes through faith in Jesus, not through human works alone. NT writers like Paul had to counteract the tendency to seek salvation by works of the law. More contemporary forms of "works righteousness" are seeking salvation through works of social justice or attempts to change the world. The Christian good news is that God has saved the world through his Son Jesus. This message of salvation will have necessary practical consequences such as social justice, but the gospel begins with preaching faith in Jesus as

the Messiah who has come to save humans from their sins and
as the Lord whom all must obey in order to come to the
Father (e.g., Acts 2:21, 36). The sins from which Jesus saves us
are both personal and social; the commands of Jesus as Lord
cover both personal and social morality, as had been so richly
demonstrated already in OT directives. But the preaching focus
is on Jesus as both Savior and Lord. ╱

The phrase translated "And now, behold" introduces the
next main subsection of the speech in verse 22:

> And now, behold, I am going to Jerusalem, bound in the
> Spirit, not knowing what shall befall me there; except that
> the Holy Spirit testifies to me in every city that imprison-
> ment and afflictions await me. But I do not account my life
> of any value nor as precious to myself, if only I may ac-
> complish my course and the ministry which I received from
> the Lord Jesus, to testify to the gospel of the grace of God
> (vv 22-24).

By predictions of the speaker's impending suffering, farewell
addresses commonly indicate that the speaker will soon be
separated from the listeners. This prediction is the third farewell element. The predictions in this speech situate Paul's
coming persecutions within God's plan as directed and foretold
by the Holy Spirit. In the Johannine farewell, Jesus tells his
disciples that he has warned them beforehand of his sufferings
lest they be a stumbling block to their faith (e.g., Jn 13:19).
Similar predictions by Paul in this speech have a comparable
narrative function of reducing the shock of his final afflictions.
Not only has the Spirit told Paul about them beforehand, but
he has accepted them willingly, without morbidly clinging to
his life. His only concern as he faced persecution and death
was accomplishing the mission given him by Jesus.

By referring to his ministry in the context of his self-
sacrificing death, Paul heightens its value. That ministry was
given to Paul by the risen Lord Jesus himself (as Paul's letters
also repeatedly insist, e.g., Gal 1:1, 15-17):

> Paul an apostle not from men or through man, but through
> Jesus Christ and God the Father, who raised him from the

> dead—.... But when he who had set me apart before I was
> born, and had called me through his grace, was pleased to
> reveal his Son to me, in order that I might preach him
> among the Gentiles, I did not confer with flesh and blood,
> nor did I go up to Jerusalem to those who were apostles
> before me, but I went away into Arabia; and again I
> returned to Damascus.

Paul's ministry, and by implication that of Christian pastors to
succeed him, is primarily to bear witness to the good news of
God's grace.

The good news of grace refers to God's sending of his Son
Jesus to die and rise for the sins of all humans (Acts 10:34-43).

> Truly I perceive that God shows no partiality, but in every
> nation any one who fears him and does what is right is
> acceptable to him. You know the word which he sent to
> Israel ... how God anointed Jesus of Nazareth with the
> Holy Spirit and with power.... They put him to death by
> hanging him on a tree; but God raised him on the third day
> and made him manifest.... To him all the prophets bear
> witness that every one who believes in him receives for-
> giveness of sins through his name.

According to Acts, that grace is primarily experienced through
the promised Holy Spirit, who comes to those who repent of
their sins and accept Jesus as their messianic savior and as
their Lord (e.g., Acts 2:38, 2:21). "And Peter said to them,
'Repent, and be baptized every one of you in the name of
Jesus Christ for the forgiveness of your sins; and you shall
receive the gift of the Holy Spirit'" (2:38). "And it shall be that
whoever calls on the name of the Lord shall be saved" (2:21).
This Spirit empowers change in Christians' own lives and gives
the courage and ability to evangelize others, as it did for the
first community at Pentecost (Acts 1-2). The Christian ministry
is primarily to spread the good news of God's mercy to the
fallen human race, by saving it through the death and resurrection of Jesus and through the bestowal of God's Holy
Spirit upon all who accept this salvation.

This good news is robbed of its urgency if people are unaware of the problem it solves—the problem of human sin and humanity's fallen condition and alienation from God, which are more explicitly described in Paul's own letters than in Acts. The NT principally announces our salvation from sin. Nowhere does the NT describe the problem from which God saves us in Jesus Christ as *primarily* one of unjust social structures. The problem Jesus died for is fundamentally that of human sin and alienation from God. Questions of unjust social structures flow from this basic problem. The Christian preacher portrayed by Acts proclaims that God saves all humans from their own sins and from the fallen state of alienation from God into which they were born and from which they are helpless to extricate themselves. The NT proclamation consistently focuses on God's grace, on human salvation from sin, death, and hell through the death and resurrection of Jesus and the sending of the Holy Spirit, which reconcile us to the Father (e.g., Acts 2:22-24, 32-39). Preaching works of love and justice flows from this basic message, and without this foundation it lacks the proper context and empowerment by God's Spirit and grace. This is the basic message and ministry to which Paul's farewell refers (Acts 20:24): "But I do not account my life of any value nor as precious to myself, if only I may accomplish my course and the ministry which I received from the Lord Jesus, to testify to the gospel of the grace of God" (v 24).

The next occurrence of "And now, behold" in verse 25 begins another main subsection of the farewell speech. Its primary focus is on the false teaching that will afflict the Christian churches after Paul's death.

> And now, behold, I know that all you among whom I have gone preaching the kingdom will see my face no more. Therefore I testify to you this day that I am innocent of the blood of all of you, for I did not shrink from declaring to you the whole counsel of God. Take heed to yourself and to all the flock, in which the Holy Spirit has made you overseers, to care for the church of God which he obtained with the blood of his own Son. I know that after my departure fierce wolves will come in among you, not sparing the flock; and from among your own selves will arise men speaking

perverse things, to draw away the disciples after them. Therefore be alert, remembering that for three years I did not cease night or day to admonish every one with tears (vv 25-31).

This subsection includes several farewell elements: no. 3—allusion to Paul's death; no. 4—declaration of Paul's innocence and fulfillment of his responsibilities; no. 5—prediction of false teachers and apostasy after Paul's death; no. 6— exhortation to pastor the church faithfully as Paul did.

Paul's allusion to his death (no. 3) sets the stage for the other three farewell elements (nos. 4-6), which share a common concern for overseeing that the full unadulterated gospel be preached. Paul's declaration that he has fulfilled the responsibilities of his ministry, his prediction of false teaching after his death, and his exhortation to pastor the church faithfully introduce two concepts that are especially important for contemporary Christianity—the biblical image of the watchman and the NT concept of "overseers" (from the same Greek word later used for "bishops").

Ezekiel 3:16-21 and 33:1-9 had spoken of the prophet as *watchman* responsible to warn Israel of God's threatened punishment for their sins.

> Son of man, I have made you a watchman for the house of Israel; whenever you hear a word from my mouth, you shall give them warning from me. If I say to the wicked, "You shall surely die," and you give him no warning, nor speak to warn the wicked from his wicked way, in order to save his life, that wicked man shall die in his iniquity; but his blood I will require at your hand. But if you warn the wicked, and he does not turn from his wickedness ... he shall die in his iniquity; but you will have saved your life.... (Ezek 3:17-19, cf. Isa 21:6: "Go, set a watchman, let him announce what he sees"; Jer 6:17: "I set watchmen over you, saying, 'Give heed to the sound of the trumpet!' but they said, 'We will not give heed.'")

The prophet, and Paul after him, is responsible for passing on God's warnings to sinners, for God wants not the death but the conversion of the sinner (Ezek 33:11: "As I live, says the Lord God, I have no pleasure in the death of the wicked, but that the wicked turn back from his way and live; turn back, turn back from your evil ways; for why will you die, O house of Israel?"; cf. Ezek 18:23, 32).

When Paul declares, "Therefore I testify to you this day that I am innocent of the blood of all of you, for I did not shrink from declaring to you the whole counsel of God" (Acts 20:26-27), he is alluding to this watchman image. If the watchman fails to warn the people, he is guilty of their blood, but if he does warn them and they choose not to heed him, their blood is their own responsibility. Since Paul has warned the Ephesians of the things that bring God's wrath, he is innocent of their blood if they fail to respond and be saved.

The purpose of preaching about God's wrath is not to frighten nor be negative or judgmental but to warn people of the consequences of their sin so they might turn away from it and repent and be converted to God's ways. This continues to be true today. Preaching God's wrath about sin should proceed from both God's and the preacher's love of sinners and desire for their reconciliation with the Father who is waiting for their return (Lk 15:20-24).

Preaching God's wrath is also meant to protect the innocent victims of sin, social injustice and abortion. God protects the lowly and helpless (Luke 1:51-52) when his law restrains the mighty from oppressive and deadly acts against them: "He has scattered the proud in the imagination of their hearts, he has put down the mighty from their thrones, and exalted those of low degree" (Luke 1:51-52). Some of the main targets of prophetic warnings were sins of social injustice, of putting other gods (which take the contemporary forms of money, sex and power) before him, and of personal and relational sins. God desires the salvation of all humans, but he is a holy God who has to cleanse the unclean and sanctify the unholy for them to be able to live forever in union with him (cf. Ezek 36:25-28, Acts 11:2-18). Therefore one of the chief roles of the prophetic "watchman" is to warn the people of their sins so they will convert and let God save them from those sins. The Acts 20 speech also applies the image of watchman to the Christian preacher and leader.

The watchman image brings home the consequences of sin and the urgency for Christian teachers and preachers to warn people of them. God does not usually spare people from the natural consequences of their free choices to sin. If Christian pastors do not warn people about the sinfulness and harmful consequences of certain behavior, both in this life (*the damage done*) and in the next (eternal loss of God's love), they will die in their sin. But God will hold those Christian leaders and teachers responsible who did not warn them that this behavior, which is condoned and even promoted by the world, is grievously offensive to God. This seems especially the case when children are not given proper moral guidance and find themselves without religious and community support to counteract intense pressure to sin from peers and environment and their own chaotic desires.

Another concept in this subsection of the speech (vv 25-31) which has special contemporary importance is the ministry of the elders as *overseers* responsible for guarding the people against false teachings. The elders are to protect their flock against both false teachers who, like wolves from outside, attack their faith, and even against some of their own number who will begin subverting the message to draw disciples away (vv 28-30). The expression *episkopoi* ("overseers") is also translated "bishops" elsewhere, as in the pastoral letters (1 Tim 3:2, Tit 1:7). This speech combines the expression "overseers" with the Gospel images of shepherding the flock and protecting it against wolves, even those in sheep's clothing (cf. the saying of Jesus in Mt 7:15). The same combination of the root *episcop—* ("oversee") with shepherding the flock occurs in 1 Peter 5:2 ("Shepherd the flock of God among you, overseeing it not by constraint but willingly...." [my literal translation]).[33] The same verbal combination of shepherd and *episkopos* appears in 1 Peter 2:25, applied to Christ as "shepherd and guardian [overseer] of your souls."

The imagery of Christian leaders and elders as *overseers* guarding their flock against the false teaching of wolves (from

---

[33]In this verse, 1 Pet 5:2, *episkopountes*, "overseeing [it]," is not textually certain but probable; cf. *TCGNT* 695-96.

outside the church) or wolves in sheep's clothing (from inside the church) has a broad base in other parts of the NT besides Acts, especially in the Gospel sayings of Jesus and in the Pauline and Petrine letter traditions. These images of overseeing the flock point to a virtually universal NT directive that warns Christian leaders to guard their churches against false teachings from without and/or within. Doctrinal supervision was clearly one of the major responsibilities of Church leaders (especially those whom the NT and early patristic writings called bishops and elders). Though this emphasis may sound strange today, it underlines how important revelation is in Christianity. It is a religion whose definitive revelation took place in the person and history of Jesus Christ. It has no new revelation beyond the good news that the Father sent his Son to die and rise in order to reconcile us with him. Because the gospel which God has revealed to the Church must be passed on faithfully to future generations, Church leaders must guard against perversions of this gospel.

In the farewell address, Paul tells the elders to be vigilant in caring for the flock over which the Holy Spirit has placed them as overseers to pastor God's Church (Acts 20:28). Since God has bought this Church at the cost of the blood of his own [Son],[34] the elders are not to let that blood be shed for their people in vain. Paul warns them that after he is gone (after the apostolic age), false teachers will not spare the flock, and even some Christian leaders will pervert the apostolic message to draw disciples away from Christ to themselves (vv 29-30). Therefore they are to be on the watch (a possible further allusion to the image of the night watchman), remembering Paul's own example of admonishing each sinner during his three years among them (v 31). This section (vv 25-31) clearly emphasizes the role of Church leaders as guardians

---

[34]The phrase *dia tou haimatos tou idiou* has the usual sense of "through his own blood," which is problematic if "his" refers to God. This reading has the best early manuscript support but the majority of later manuscripts and the Byzantine lectionary read *idiou haimatos* along with a previous variant of "Lord and God" for "God." However, none of these changes are necessary if one understands the best attested phrase, *dia tou haimatos tou idiou*, as "through the blood of his own" which is justified by the absolute use in contemporary papyri of *ho idios* as "his own" for close relatives. *TCGNT* 480-82.

of the apostolic tradition and Church teaching, and their duty
to admonish anyone who goes or leads others astray in doctrine or behavior.

The expression "and now" indicates the transition in verse
32 to the final section of the speech.

> And now I commend you to God and to the word of his
> grace, which is able to build you up and to give you the
> inheritance among all those who are sanctified. I coveted no
> one's silver or gold or apparel. You yourselves know that
> these hands ministered to my necessities, and to those who
> were with me. In all things I have shown you that by so
> toiling one must help the weak, remembering the words of
> the Lord Jesus, how he said, 'It is more blessed to give than
> to receive' (vv 32-35).

The final section of the Acts 20 speech features the seventh
and second farewell elements listed at the beginning of this
chapter. Paul's commending the elders to God is a standard
element (no. 7) in farewell discourses. He also commends them
to the message of God's grace (the gospel), which God uses to
build them up and bring them to heaven (v 32). This final
section also returns to the second farewell element, imitation
of Paul's example. Thus Paul begins and ends his farewell by
pointing to himself as a model for later Church leaders to
follow.

Paul also includes additional elements of apologetic for his
ministry beyond those in the fourth farewell element above.
His self-defense in verses 33-35 against all possible charges of
greed or abusing his office for his own aggrandizement has
precedents in biblical farewells, such as Samuel's speech when
he announces the first king, Saul (1 Sam 12:3-5):

> "Here I am; testify against me before the Lord and before
> his anointed. Whose ox have I taken? or whose ass have I
> taken? Or whom have I defrauded? Whom have I oppres-
> sed? Or from whose hand have I taken a bribe to blind my
> eyes with it? Testify against me and I will restore it to you."
> They said, "You have not defrauded us or oppressed us or
> taken anything from any man's hand." And he said to

them, "The Lord is witness against you, and his anointed is witness this day, that you have not found anything in my hand." And they said, "He is witness."

Samuel's innocence contrasts with the abuse of priestly power by Eli's sons, who were condemned during Samuel's youth (1 Sam 2:12-17, 22-25 and 3:11-14). Samuel's refusal to abuse his authority was one of the strongest signs of the integrity of his service as judge, whereas accumulating wealth for himself at the expense of his subjects would have besmirched the good memory of his term of office.

Paul's echo of Samuel's protest of innocence in his farewell address emphasized his view that Christian authority is for the service of God and the people, not for one's own advantage. The critical importance of this for Christian ministry has shown itself over and again in the history of the Church, when the wealth of Church leaders has scandalized the faithful, and the poverty of saints has given credibility to their work. Paul's answer is simple but eloquent: he has not sought anyone else's goods even for his genuine needs as he ministered to them, but he worked with his own hands to supply the needs of himself and his co-workers.

As guidance for the Ephesian elders, Paul points both to his example of working to help the weak and to the memory of Jesus' words, thus indicating at least two sources of authority for Christian exhortation. One is the speaker's example. The other is the recollection of sayings of Jesus as having the highest authority for Church life. This particular saying, "it is more blessed to give than to receive" (v 35), is not extant in the Gospels. Even if it did not to go back to Jesus, its citation here indicates that Christians at the end of the first century still had recourse to sayings of Jesus independent of Gospel contexts.[35] Apparently there still existed collections of sayings of Jesus apart from the Gospels on which speechwriters could and did draw for authoritative exhortation.

---

[35]Cf. Schneider, *Apostelgeschichte* 2.299, bibliography p 291; H. Koester, *Introduction to the New Testament. Vol 2: History and Literature of Early Christianity* (Foundations and Facets; Philadelphia: Fortress, 1982) 67-68 describes the use of extra-Gospel sayings of Jesus into the second century.

8-9
Final Prayer
+
Farewell
Gestures

The last two farewell elements (nos. 8-9), Paul's and the elders' prayer and farewell gestures, provide the narrative conclusion after the speech, just as the first element, Paul's summons of the elders for the speech, furnishes its introduction. Most narratives present parting words and gestures at the conclusion of farewell speeches. Acts 20:36-38 shows Paul praying with those he addressed, their parting gestures of grief and love for Paul, and their sorrow especially at his statement that they would never see his face again. Finally the elders accompany him to the ship on which he would sail out of their lives. This ending adds to the poignancy of the situation of leave-taking in which the speech is set. Paul's concern that Christian leaders preach and preserve the complete Christian revelation takes on added importance, both for the elders in the narrative and for later readers.

NB The primary function of the biblical version of the farewell address genre is to describe and promote transition from original religious leaders like Jesus, Moses, David, and Paul to their successors. It is especially concerned with maintaining community tradition and the authority to preserve that tradition for later generations. The very genre has a conservative aspect to it. It is not primarily concerned with progressive unfolding of the tradition nor with adapting it to changing circumstances. Since these are also important, the farewell genre can appear a bit one-sided in not dealing with them. The fairly pure example of the genre in Acts 20 does nothing to mitigate this one-sided emphasis on tradition and authority. Other farewell addresses like John 13-17 balance this traditional emphasis by stressing also the Holy Spirit's continued presence with future generations to lead them to deeper awareness of truths which disciples during Jesus' lifetime were unable to understand.

The very one-sidedness of Acts 20's farewell address can have its own contemporary importance, however, as a counterbalance for some current exaggerations. Acts 20 tempers individualism with the responsibility of Church leaders to guard the basic apostolic tradition. It reminds them to warn against sin and to correct those who go astray. It counters religious relativism with the duty of Christian preachers to proclaim Jesus as saving Messiah and Lord of all. The farewell speech warns Church leaders and preachers against personal aggrandizement or being corrupted by their access to power and wealth. Through Paul's example it asks them to live personal lives of gospel poverty, and urges them to self-sacrifice, even to the point of martyrdom, in fidelity to their evangelizing mission.

Finally, God's steward brings out from the storehouse of revelation things old and new, traditional and reformist. Although Paul's farewell has primarily a traditional and conserving purpose, as God's word it cannot be reduced to a conservative ideology. God's word is "sharper than any two-edged sword, piercing to the division of soul and spirit, of joints and marrow, and discerning the thoughts and intentions of the heart" (Heb 4:12). It convicts the conscience of all parties. In its different genres, Scripture addresses the human condition of the Church in all ages, which involves both sin and forgiveness, authority and love, warning and hope, preservation of apostolic truth and self-sacrificing generosity for one's people. Whether popular or not, Acts 20 remains one important canonical voice for all ages.

2

Luke 22

Viewing Luke's presentation of the last supper as a farewell address increases the poignancy of the narrative. In his last meal with his apostles, Jesus gives them in the Eucharist a way to render his saving death sacramentally present to future generations. He prepares them for their own betrayal, denial and abandonment of him and for a way to repent and be restored to favor afterward. He corrects their misunderstandings of authority and places them in authority over the restored Israel despite their shortcomings, with Simon over them all. He warns them to be ready for increased hostility after his death and resurrection. The scene ends with Jesus going to face his death alone because they temporarily misunderstand him. Until recently, few writers have referred to Luke 22:14-38 as a farewell address.[36] Most have instead asked questions about the institution of the Eucharist, text critical questions or questions about which of the sayings go back to the historical Jesus.[37] For example, one book about last words in ancient narratives treats not Luke 22:14-38 but rather Luke 23:46, "Father, into thy hands I commit my spirit!"[38] Yet if Luke 22

---

[36]Kurz, "Luke 22:14-38," 251-253. J. Neyrey, *The Passion According to Luke: A Redaction Study of Luke's Soteriology* (Theological Inquiries; New York: Paulist, 1985) 5-48 does treat Luke 22:14-38 as a farewell speech.

[37]Ibid., 252, n 4. E.g., J. A. Fitzmyer, *The Gospel According to Luke (X-XXIV)* (AB 28A; Garden City, Doubleday, 1985) 2.1385-1406 does not treat Luke 22:14-38 primarily as a farewell address (though he mentions in passing that Luke combines Jesus' words at the last supper in the form of a farewell discourse, p 1386, and refers to a final discourse on pp 1408-1409) but deals with verses 15-20 as "The Last Supper," and form critically as a story about Jesus.

[38]W. Schmidt, *De Ultimis Morientium Verbis* (Diss., U. Marburg; Marburg: Chr. Schaaf, 1914) 64.

is read as a farewell address, many of its puzzles are solved, because it fits the farewell pattern, a pattern that unifies and focuses the diverse content of these traditional sayings of Jesus.

As always, I will deal primarily with the final canonical state of the text rather than with questions about its possible sources. Even questions about which manuscripts to follow in establishing the text will be handled from the perspective of the canonical and liturgical uses of these passages through the ages.

The following standard farewell elements appear in this order: predictions of death, directions for actions after one's death, predictions that followers will defect, instructions for succession, choices of successors and naming authorities among the group, predictions of future trials and directions to meet them, and misunderstanding by disciples. This farewell structure gives coherence to the passage, focusing everything in it on Jesus' provisions for his impending death. Thus he provides for his departure in the following ways: (1) Jesus predicts that this will be his last meal before his death. (2) He gives his apostles the Eucharist ("my body given for you ... the new covenant in my blood which is shed for you") [my literal translation], and asks them to "Do this in memory of me." (3) He predicts that one of them will betray him, and they ask among themselves who it will be. (4) They dispute about who is the greatest, and Jesus uses this opportunity to teach them the true meaning of Christian authority as service. (5) After teaching his meaning of authority, he places them in authority in his kingdom over the twelve tribes of Israel. (6) Jesus warns Simon he will deny him but gives him the mission (and authority) to "strengthen your brethren" after his repentance. (7) He warns the apostles they will encounter hostility in their mission after his death and changes his previous directions about how to prepare for it. (8) The dialogue ends when the disciples misunderstand Jesus and take his mention of swords literally.

The most significant of these elements for the implied readers are the Eucharist and the meaning of Christian authority. My discussion will follow the order and format of the farewell address genre, but it will emphasize Luke's treatment of Eucharist and Christian authority.

Many commentators and even some manuscript copyists have been puzzled by the apparent progression of cup, bread, cup in what they saw as an obviously eucharistic context. For the Eucharist, the two mentions of the cup and the apparent inversion of the proper liturgical order of bread-cup seemed abnormalities.[39] The farewell structure enables the reader to separate the first mention of the cup from the eucharistic context and to see it as a separate and previous element. It predicts Jesus' imminent death by referring to his last passover and the last cup of wine he would drink before the coming of God's kingdom.

The farewell address passage begins with a reference to "the hour" arriving. This could be a simple reference to suppertime (cf. Lk 14:17, "and at the time [literally, 'hour'] for the banquet he sent his servant...."), but seems also to share some of the Johannine connotations of Jesus' "hour" (Jn 2:4; 7:30; 8:20; 12:23-27; 17:1; esp. 13:1, "when Jesus knew that his hour had come to depart ... to the Father").[40] In Luke's account of his arrest, Jesus uses the term in a "Johannine" sense: "When I was with you day after day in the temple, you did not lay hands on me. But this is your hour, and the power of darkness" (Lk 22:53). This has striking similarities to John 7:30, "So they thought to arrest him; but no one laid hands on him, because his hour had not yet come," and to the Johannine theme of darkness (Jn 1:5; 8:12; 12:35, 38; and 13:30 "It was night").

"The hour" can imply a sense of God's timing for what is about to occur (cf. Lk 7:21; 10:21; 12:12, 40, 46; 13:31). In these Lukan passages, "the hour" acts not only as a narrative transition and setting, but seems also to have connotations of the hour of revelation, miracles, trials, testing or unexpected appearance of the Son of Man. For example, when the questioners from the Baptist ask whether Jesus is the expected one (Lk 7:20), the narrator interjects the following before Jesus'

---

[39] *TCGNT* 173-177; Fitzmyer, *Luke X-XXIV*, 2.1388, 1397-98.

[40] Many scholars have been impressed by the striking resonances between the Gospel of John and peculiarly Lukan material. See J. Fitzmyer, *The Gospel According to Luke (I-IX)* (AB 28; Garden City: Doubleday, 1981) 87-88 with bibliography p 104; R. Maddox, *The Purpose of Luke-Acts* (FRLANT 126; Göttingen: Vandenhoeck & Ruprecht, 1982) 158-79 (ch 6, "The Special Affinities of Luke and John").

answer: "In that hour he cured many of diseases and plagues and evil spirits..." (Lk 7:21). After Jesus tells the seventy to rejoice that their names are written in heaven (Lk 10:20), the narrator continues, "In that same hour he rejoiced in the Holy Spirit and said, 'I thank thee, Father ... that thou hast hidden these things from the wise and understanding..." (Lk 10:21). In this passage, the occurrence of "the hour" alludes to salvation history as well as to the time of day: "And when the hour came, he sat at table, and the apostles with him" (Lk 22:14). Jesus' reference to his death at the very beginning of his farewell heightens the portentous aspects of the opening clause, "And when the hour came." He begins by stating his earnest desire to eat this passover with them before his death. He predicts he will not eat it again until it is fulfilled in God's kingdom (vv 15-16).

Jesus' farewell meal has a passover setting. His reference to fulfilling the passover would probably have sounded mysterious to the disciples at the time, but it has obvious symbolism for later Christian readers. Although the fulfillment of passover is partially seen in the Christian Eucharist itself, it refers ultimately to the redemption of God's people at Jesus' second coming when God's kingdom will appear in its full power and manifestation (cf. Lk 21:25-31). As the first passover commemorated how God saved his people from the Egyptians, the final or eschatological fulfillment of the passover will take place only when God's kingdom is fully present, when the Son of Man returns in power to bring definitive salvation to God's people.

> And then they will see the Son of man coming in a cloud with power and great glory. Now when these things begin to take place, look up and raise your heads, because your redemption is drawing near (Lk 21:27-28).

Only then will Christians be fully vindicated.

The first reference to the cup seems to be a traditional saying inherited by Luke.[41] It sounds like a eucharistic ex-

---

[41]Cf. Fitzmyer, *Luke X-XXIV* 2.1397.

pression, whose apparent redundancy with the eucharistic cup has caused much confusion among later readers. "And he took a cup, and when he had given thanks he said, 'Take this, and divide it among yourselves'" (v 17). Although this has a eucharistic ring, the rest of the saying does not have any of the standard liturgical formulae for the Eucharist. "For I tell you that from now on I shall not drink of the fruit of the vine until the kingdom of God comes" (v 18). This saying does not relate to Eucharist but to a poignant foretelling of Jesus' death that resonates with his reference to eating the passover one last time. In this context, that is its main function.

Despite Luke's incorporation of the first wine saying into a non-eucharistic farewell, its balance with the passover statement was likely to confuse Christian readers. The original combination of the statement by Jesus, "I have earnestly desired to eat this passover with you before I suffer," (v 15) with his taking a cup of wine and adding, "Take this, and divide it among yourselves" (v 17), probably did have eucharistic connotations. For Christians would find a natural link between the Eucharist and a new passover. [42] Certainly the eucharistic reference to "the new covenant in my blood" would carry passover implications for Christians. The Israelites associated passover with their covenant in blood because the blood of the lamb on their doors saved them in Egypt. Similarly, the new covenant in the blood of Jesus, to whom Christians referred as Lamb of God (Jn 1:29, 36, Rev 5:6, 12, and often; cf. Acts 8:32), would carry passover associations. The difference between the original eucharistic connotations of the passover and wine sayings, and their incorporation by Luke for non-eucharistic farewell functions, probably caused confusion. Luke's further addition of specifically eucharistic formulae only added to the confusion of both scribes and commentators over the seemingly double reference to the eucharistic cup. Nevertheless, the present Lukan context clearly uses the first passover and wine sayings for a non-eucharistic purpose, to express Jesus' prediction of his imminent death in the setting of his farewell address.

---

[42] Cf. Fitzmyer, *Luke X-XXIV*, 2.1389-92.

The farewell context then leads directly to the properly eucharistic sayings in verses 19-20.

> And he took bread, and when he had given thanks he broke it and gave it to them saying, "This is my body, which is given for you. Do this in remembrance of me." And likewise the cup after supper, saying, "This cup which is poured out for you is the new covenant in my blood."

How appropriately the Eucharist fits the farewell setting. The bread symbolizes Jesus' coming death; the cup signifies the new covenant with another allusion to his death (in his blood "poured out for you"). Jesus tells the disciples to "do this in my memory," which is a most appropriate instruction for a farewell speech. His giving of the Eucharist clearly points to his coming sacrificial death on their behalf. It is a new covenant or testament which he establishes just before his death, which will change the relationship between his disciples and God. Jesus' command to "do this in my memory" initiates their regular repetition of the Eucharist after his death. The Eucharist functions as a lasting memorial to Jesus and his death. All these aspects of the Eucharist fit Jesus' farewell and provision for his followers after his death.

Textual problems with these verses, however, have distracted scholars from noticing how well they fit the farewell genre. The two main variants which explain all the other textual variations are the full text printed in most Bibles and implied in this analysis, and a much shorter variant peculiar to one major Western manuscript and some Old Latin versions, which leaves out verses 19b-20. The Western version reads in my literal translation:

> And accepting the cup, having given thanks, he said, "Take this, divide it among yourselves. For I tell you from now on I will not drink from the fruit of the vine until the kingdom of God comes." And taking bread, having blessed it he broke and gave it to them saying, "This is my body."[43]

---

[43]Translated from *TCGNT*, 175.

This short text presents an inverted order of cup before bread so problematic that several other Old Latin and Syriac manuscripts reversed it.[44] The short text retains some farewell emphasis, such as the statement Jesus will not drink wine again until the coming of God's kingdom, with its implied prediction of Jesus' death. But it loses the explicit reference to Jesus' body given for us and blood shed for us and the command to do this in his memory. Nor does it refer to the new covenant.

Some translators and commentators have preferred this shorter variant, thinking the addition sounded more like 1 Corinthians 11:24b-25 than like Luke's style. Most now accept the longer account as Lukan, since the textual evidence is so overwhelmingly in its favor. The similarity with Paul and the non-Lukan style and theology probably stem from Lukan familiarity with the eucharistic formulae in the Pauline churches which he describes in Acts.[45] This analysis accepts the longer text as genuine, both on textual grounds[46] and in the light of the usually overlooked evidence from the farewell genre. An added reason for analyzing the longer text is that it is the canonical one used by the Church and theologians for centuries, which was not significantly questioned until the Enlightenment.

In the full received text (Lk 22:19-20), Jesus gives the apostles the Eucharist with the liturgical formulae of the Pauline churches, as can be seen by comparison to 1 Corinthians:

> ...that the Lord Jesus on the night when he was betrayed took bread, and when he had given thanks, he broke it, and said, "This is my body which is for you. Do this in remembrance of me." In the same way also the cup, after supper, saying, "This cup is the new covenant in my blood. Do this, as often as you drink it, in remembrance of me" (1 Cor 11:23-25).

[44]Ibid., 174.
[45]Ibid., 176-177; cf. Fitzmyer, *Luke X-XXIV*, 2.1387-88.
[46]So Fitzmyer, *Luke X-XXIV*, 2.1388.

Luke 22:19-20 follows this same order of taking bread, giving thanks, breaking and giving it to them. The eucharistic words are almost identical with Paul's: "This is my body, which is given for you. Do this in remembrance of me" (Lk 22:19). The transition to the cup also echoes Paul: "And likewise the cup after supper, saying..." (Lk 22:20). Finally a literal translation of the Lukan words over the wine closely resemble Paul's: "This cup is the new covenant in my blood which is shed for you" (Lk 22:20). The expression about blood "which is shed for you" goes beyond the Pauline cup formula, but in a way that closely parallels the Pauline bread formula, "my body which is for you." Luke also lacks the second command to do this in Christ's memory.

The giving of the Eucharist greatly enriches the farewell dimensions of Jesus' speech in Luke. The breaking of the bread foreshadows the breaking of Jesus' physical body in his passion and death. He gives his disciples his own body and blood in complete and literal self-sacrifice. (Though John's Gospel lacks this passage, it has a corresponding statement at this point in the narrative, "Greater love has no man than this, that a man lay down his life for his friends" [Jn 15:13]). He asks his disciples to "do this" in eucharistic commemoration of him, instituting a practice that would memorialize him throughout Church history. (In fact, one purpose of this Lukan account is to ground the Christian liturgical celebration of the Eucharist in Jesus' last supper.)[47] In the eucharistic words recited today by the bishop or priest in place of Jesus and by his instructions, Jesus continues to give his body and his blood as a sacrifice for all. This eucharistic action makes present his new covenant that reconciles his followers to the Father. The Eucharist when done by Jesus at the last supper foreshadowed his historical passion, and made that passion present again when done in his stead ("Do this") by apostles and those who succeeded them after his death and resurrection. It is Jesus' ultimate gift to his followers.

For contemporary Christians, Luke's setting of the Eucharist

---

[47]Cf. Fitzmyer, 2.1395.

within Jesus' farewell address emphasizes the Eucharist as his last gift and command to his Church. As Jesus' "memorial," the Eucharist brings to every age his sacrifice of his own life for the salvation of all. The wording of the Eucharist, "This is my body which is given for you.... This cup is the new covenant in my blood which is poured out for you," emphasizes the sacrificial dimensions of Eucharist. It is not just a memorial meal, though it is done "in memory of me." The statement that the Eucharist is the new covenant in Jesus' blood which reconciles fallen humans with the Father stresses Christ's bloody sacrifice on our behalf. Even the treatment of Christ's body and blood as separate implies his death. At least this passage gives no support to some contemporary liturgical tendencies to treat the Eucharist as only a celebratory meal rather than as a memorial of Christ's sacrifice.

Nor is the focus in this passage primarily on the Eucharist as community meal, with the corresponding liturgical emphasis on "horizontal" expressions of community. The farewell setting in Luke focuses the Eucharist not on the community but on Jesus and his saving act. The Eucharist is to be done "in memory of me," not "in celebration of you." The farewell setting thus provides a corrective to one-sided swings of the liturgical pendulum away from Eucharist as sacrifice toward community meal only. It also serves as a reminder of the reverence and solemnity which remembering Jesus' death deserves. It can help restore the insides of churches as places to pray to God and not just socialize with others. It puts the focus on God and Christ instead of merely celebration with the community, though that too should be provided for, as in churches with ante-rooms for socializing behind the place of worship.

Christians have always experienced the Eucharist in the light of Jesus' resurrection as well as his death. By his narrative setting of the first Eucharist in a solemn farewell address focusing on Jesus' impending death, Luke reminds Christians of every age what the Eucharist cost Jesus. The farewell setting recalls that Jesus' sacrificial death makes resurrection possible, and forestalls the perennial human temptation toward a "theology of glory," sometimes colloquially referred to as "cheap grace."[47a] The Eucharist is not just a celebration after the resurrection. The eucharistic words recall primarily Jesus' sacrificial death.

Nor is the Eucharist just a meal that builds community. It is Jesus' action of giving his body and blood to his Church through his apostles and their successors who "do this in memory of me." Although the Eucharist does promote unity among Christians, it accomplishes this by uniting individuals sacramentally with the body and blood of Jesus—a meal uniting the whole community primarily with Jesus, and because of that with each other.

Finally, the Lukan setting of the Eucharist in Jesus' farewell to the twelve apostles (Lk 22:14, 30) puts a special focus on the apostles and on their successors. Most farewell addresses focus especially on those leaders who will succeed the dying founder, emphasizing their special roles and tasks with respect to the rest of the community. Luke 22 is no exception to this. The Lukan farewell address places special focus on the twelve apostles as successors to Jesus, who reenact the Eucharist in his stead and who exercise his authority over the restored people of God.[48] As the original Lukan readers listened to their elders say in the Sunday Eucharist, "This is my body," they would have spontaneously identified this as the continuation of the function given to the apostles in Jesus' farewell, to "do this in memory of me." So have Christians to this day.

Jesus' farewell takes on a special poignancy in the jarring transition from his eucharistic self-sacrifice to his betrayal by one of the very twelve apostles to whom he has entrusted so much. The betrayal is the worse because that apostle had shared Jesus' table: "But behold the hand of him who betrays me is on the table" (Lk 22:21). In first century Palestine, table fellowship was not shared casually, as in contemporary fast

---

[47a]"The irony is that Luke is often accused of having a "theology of glory," though Fitzmyer, among others, objects to that interpretation (*Luke I-IX*, 22-23, bibliography pp 29-34).

[48]For the twelve apostles as authorities over the restored Israel, cf. L. T. Johnson, *The Writings of the New Testament: An Interpretation* (Philadelphia: Fortress, 1986) 217-19, 223-28.

food society. Psalm 41:9 expresses the agony of such betrayal: "Even my bosom friend in whom I trusted, who ate of my bread, has lifted his heel against me." Nor did the apostle betray only the table of ordinary hospitality; he has just shared the table of the first Eucharist! Jesus warns that although he is walking the road decreed by God for the Son of Man, "woe to that man by whom he is betrayed!" (Lk 22:22). Jesus is submitting to the Father's plan, which can appear inscrutable to humans: as he will die for the worthy and unworthy, so he has given his Eucharist to the worthy and unworthy. But woe to the unworthy Judas. Judas is acting with the freedom all humans have, but he will soon have to bear the terrible consequences of his betraying Christ. Jesus' warning to his betrayer fails to change his resolve. Instead of repenting, Judas joins the other apostles in asking to whom he was referring (v 23).

Some might find it implausible that in this solemn farewell setting the dispute about who is the greatest should have erupted. Recognizing the similarity of this pericope to the disputes over greatness in Matthew and Mark, which took place during Jesus' public ministry (Mk 10:41-45, Mt 20:24-28), critics find the setting in those Gospels more likely. But Tannehill shows how natural the progression is from initial defensiveness to comparisons of superiority.[49] Other biblical narratives corroborate this progression. When God questioned Adam and Eve in Genesis about their guilt, they destroyed their God-given unity by refusing to accept responsibility for their own sin as Adam turned against Eve (Gen 3:7-12). The Pharisee in Luke who did not admit his sin but placed himself above others exhibits the same fallen human tendency toward comparisons (Lk 18:10-12). This passage emphasizes the apostles' shortcomings on the eve of Jesus' death, which makes the contrast in Acts with their post-Pentecost heroism all the more striking.[50]

Because the dispute is so jarring, Jesus' answer becomes all

---

[49]R. Tannehill, *The Narrative Unity of Luke-Acts: A Literary Interpretation,* vol. 1: The Gospel according to Luke (Foundations and Facets; Philadelphia: Fortress, 1986) 263.

[50]Ibid., 263- 65.

the more memorable. After prophesying his death and giving the apostles the Eucharist and before placing them in authority over the restored Israel, Jesus teaches them the true meaning of Christian authority. It is service, not domination and self-aggrandizement like gentile kingship. Christian authorities are to act as slaves, as the least in society. Jesus points to his own example as decisive: "But I am among you as one who serves" (v 27). This lesson runs directly counter to contemporary attitudes towards authority. Even though many Christians repeat the NT statements that authority is service, their actions belie this claim. Christian authority *is* service, not power backed up by physical coercion or domination against people's will. Yet contemporary Church factions often are based on the shared view that Church authority is power, and that the deprivation or possession of authority means the deprivation or possession of power and human dignity. Anger at biblical commands for submission and subordination to authority can also stem from a view of authority as domination and of submission as a subservience which is beneath human dignity.

Authority is a necessary service to any community. Lack of it brings anarchy and chaos. Christians who have rightly exercised authority know from experience the huge amount of time, hard work and concern it requires. They experience it as service and are often relieved to let others take over its burdens. Christian authority requires self-abnegation, concern for others and not oneself. The service aspects of authority are found in its exercise, not in its abnegation. Leaders who do all the work themselves instead of directing the work of the whole community are not exercising authority. Authority means headship, guiding the community as a whole, delegating reponsibilities and making final decisions after proper consultation. These demanding activities are necessary for the proper functioning of the community. When exercised for the sake of the community and not for personal power or domination, they truly serve the good of the community.

Jesus himself is the model of Church authority both in his leadership and in his submission to the Father. Though he loved and respected his disciples, he clearly had the final word, and was not slow to correct their behavior or to give them commands (which he never called "suggestions"). He taught them the gospel and trained them in discipleship, so that they in turn could teach and exercise proper authority over future disciples. His use of authority was not to exercise control. Because his own authority was totally submitted to doing his Father's will, he guided his disciples to obey the Father as he did. He exercised authority by example and self-sacrifice as well as by giving commands. His ultimate act as one in authority was to die on behalf of his disciples, so that they could be saved. His authority over the Church is cited by Ephesians as a model for a husband's relationship with his wife. Husbands are to love and sacrifice their lives for their wives as Christ did for the Church (Eph 5:25) and to love them as they love themselves, for they are truly one flesh (Eph 5:28-31). Proper exercise of Christian authority is an expression of unity and service, not of individualism, power or domination. In making decisions and giving directions it seeks not to serve itself but to serve the Father and help others to do his will.

After instructing his apostles on the meaning of Christian authority, Jesus gives them authority over the twelve tribes of the restored Israel.

> You are those who have continued with me in my trials; and I assign to you, as my Father assigned to me, a kingdom, that you may eat and drink at my table in my kingdom, and sit on thrones judging the twelve tribes of Israel (Lk 22:28-30).

Providing for the community's future is a primary purpose of farewell addresses. Jesus has already given his Church the Eucharist. Now he provides successors to govern it on his behalf. Because the apostles have remained with Jesus through the trials of his ministry, he gives them a kingdom, as his Father had given it to him (Lk 22:28-29). The Greek verb used for this gift (*diatithemai*) is a cognate of the noun for a last will or covenant (*diathēkē*), and often carries connotations of making a will. Jesus is conferring authority on the apostles as his last will and testament to them. Even though they are about to fail in their fidelity to him during his passion, Jesus looks beyond their failure to their later repentance and names them his successors. Thus he cites the fall, repentance and commission of Simon Peter:

> Simon, Simon, behold, Satan demanded to have you, that he might sift you like wheat, but I have prayed for you that your faith may not fail; and when you have turned again, strengthen your brethren (vv 31-32).

When Jesus says, "I assign to you, as my Father assigned to me, a kingdom," he is naming his twelve apostles his successors in governing the twelve tribes of the restored Israel. They receive from Jesus the authority he had received from the Father. Though Acts does not explicitly narrate the continuation of this apostolic succession except in the replacement of Judas (Acts 1), it implies further succession of their authority into the later Church by stories concerning the Hellenistic "deacons" in Acts 6, apostolic confirmation of Paul's work in Acts 15, and of Paul's successors over the Ephesian church (Acts 20). The Church has traditionally interpreted Acts as implying continuity of authority from the apostles through to the elders and others who succeeded Paul at the end of Acts.[51]

Although the speech uses the primarily eschatological images of the heavenly banquet and thrones for this transfer of authority, that transfer is not limited to the end of time but also structures Church life in Acts. The apostles will eat and drink at Jesus' table in his kingdom, and sit on thrones judging the twelve tribes of Israel. Jesus had often previously used the image of a feast for eschatological fulfillment (Lk 15:22-32, 12:35-40, 13:28-29, esp. 14:12-24). Sitting at Jesus' table implies intimacy with him as well as honor for the apostles. Judging the twelve tribes is also primarily an eschatological symbol, since the ten northern tribes were dispersed with the fall of the northern kingdom of Israel and were never again political entities. The phrase, "the twelve tribes of Israel," expressed more of an eschatological hope than a reality current at the

---

[51]See "Dogmatic Constitution on the Church," *Vatican Council II: The Conciliar and Post Conciliar Documents* (2 of 4 vols. to date; Northport, NY: Costello, 1975, 1982) 1.371-72, # 20 explicitly citing Acts 20:25, 27, 28. Compare *1 Clem* 44 in *The Apostolic Fathers* (LCL; Cambridge, Mass.: Harvard, 1970 [1912]) 1.82-85.

time of Jesus. That is its sense in much of the NT as well, as at the beginning of the letter to James ("To the twelve tribes in the Dispersion," Jas 1:1) and in Revelation ("a hundred and forty-four thousand sealed, out of every tribe of the sons of Israel," Rev 7:4, cf. vv 4-10). Luke-Acts emphasizes the number twelve because of this eschatological mission of the Twelve Apostles. Peter directs the community to restore the twelfth apostleship after Judas' defection (Acts 1:15-26), to reestablish an eschatological judge for all twelve of the restored tribes of Israel. He did not have to replace James, the brother of John who was the first of the twelve to be martyred (Acts 12:2), for his martyr's death does not prevent his eschatological judgment of Israel.

Although the apostles' authority is ultimately eschatological, its exercise begins in Acts after Jesus' death and resurrection. Acts shows the apostles converting large numbers from Israel who accept Jesus as their messiah and Lord, thus beginning Israel's restoration (esp. Acts 2-3). Acts describes the confrontations between the old authorities of Israel (the Sanhedrin) and the apostles, with the new authorities winning every confrontation (esp. Acts 4-5).[52] Even the eschatological meal at Jesus' table, which is promised in Luke 22:30, is foreshadowed in Luke-Acts, when the resurrected Jesus eats with the apostles.

> And while they still disbelieved for joy, and wondered, he said to them, "Have you anything here to eat?" They gave him a piece of broiled fish, and he took it and ate before them (Lk 24:41-43).

> [God] . . . made him manifest; not to all the people but to us who were chosen by God as witnesses, who ate and drank with him after he rose from the dead (Acts 10:40b-41).

Though the purpose of those meals was primarily witness to the reality of the resurrection, the narrator may also be

---

[52]See L. T. Johnson, *The Literary Function of Possessions in Luke-Acts* (SBLDS 39; Missoula, Mont.: Scholars, 1977) 192-93.

implying some hint of fulfillment of Jesus' promise in Luke 22:30 of eschatological table fellowship with him.

Farewell commissions to groups often single out individuals for special authority (e.g., Judah in Gen 49:8-10, Simeon and Judas Maccabeus in 1 Macc 2:65-66). Here Jesus singles out Simon and gives him authority over the twelve. Though Peter had obviously exercised a leadership role among the twelve throughout much of the Gospel (e.g., when he spoke for them all in confessing Jesus as "the Christ of God" in Lk 9:20), his authority does not presume special virtue on his part as a prerequisite, for it is given in the same breath as a prediction of his denial of Jesus. Jesus begins with a solemn warning: "Simon, Simon, behold, Satan demanded to have you [plural], that he might sift you [plural] like wheat, but I have prayed for you [singular] that your faith may not fail; and when you have turned again, strengthen your brethren" (Lk 22:31-32). Satan will temporarily overcome the apostles, but Jesus prays especially for Peter that his faith not fail despite his denial. After his repentance, Peter has the commission to strengthen his brother apostles who also have fallen. This is a beautiful model for the exercise of Christian authority. Peter's own repentance enables him to strengthen others who have failed. Peter does this by witnessing to them that he has seen Jesus risen (Lk 24:34) and by ordering them to choose a twelfth to replace Judas (Acts 1:15-26). Peter incarnates a Christian authority figure who himself has repented his sins, who can witness to his personal relationship with the risen Jesus, and whose commands build up the body by providing for its needs.

Peter's authority does not rest on his own strength or virtue, but on Jesus' forgiveness, empowerment and commission. Peter's protest to Jesus that he was prepared to suffer prison and death with him was an empty boast. Jesus responded that Peter will deny knowing Jesus three times that very night (vv 33-34). Despite Peter's coming apostasy, Jesus did not withdraw Peter's commission and authority over the apostles and community. The prophecy of Peter's denial increases the ominous forewarnings characteristic of farewells before a traumatic death.

The density of the last section of this speech has puzzled some commentators. For example, why would Jesus seem to contradict his earlier directives. One remembers that when he had sent out the disciples without provisions they did not lack what they needed (Lk 9:3, cf. 10:4),[53] but now he says they should obtain provisions for themselves, and even buy a sword (vv 35-36).

> And he said to them, "When I sent you out with no purse or bag or sandals, did you lack anything?" They said, "Nothing." He said to them, "But now, let him who has a purse take it, and likewise a bag. And let him who has no sword sell his mantle and buy one. For I tell you that this scripture must be fulfilled in me, 'And he was reckoned with transgressors'; for what is written about me has its fulfill-ment." And they said, "Look, Lord, here are two swords." And he said to them, "It is enough" (Lk 22:35-38).

Some interpret this reversal as metaphorical. The disciples misunderstood Jesus by talking literally about having two swords. The command pointed symbolically to a dramatic future situation of hostility when Jesus will be "reckoned with transgressors" (Isa 53:12 in v 37). The hostility will begin at Jesus' arrest: "Have you come out as against a robber, with swords and clubs?" (Lk 22:52), and will carry over when the disciples also are "reckoned with transgressors" in Acts (e.g., "They arrested the apostles and put them in the common prison," Acts 5:18). It functions primarily as a warning about the difference between their peaceful past ministry and the hostility that awaits them in the future, not as an actual com-mand to obtain swords.[54] The change in directives could also be an indirect justification for the two different approaches used by the missionaries who supported themselves (such as Paul, Acts 20, 1 Cor 9) and those who were supported by the communities they served (as Jesus had directed in the Gospels, e.g., Lk 10:7). If so, this passage defends Paul against criticism

[53]See Fitzmyer, *Luke X-XXIV*, 2.1429-30, 843.
[54]Cf. ibid., 2.1430-35.

that he was not acting as Jesus had instructed (cf. 1 Cor 9:3-7, 12-19).[55]

One thing is clear. The disciples' response about having two swords is a misunderstanding of Jesus' point. Other farewell addresses also end on misunderstanding by disciples, as when Socrates' disciples misunderstand him at the end of his farewell dialogue in Plato's *Phaedo*. Crito's last question was "But how shall we bury you?" (*Phaedo* 115c). Socrates quipped, "Any way you like, that is, if you can catch me...." (115c). He ended the dialogue by stressing how Crito has missed his point that he, Socrates, would leave them when he died and would not be identified with his corpse (115c-e). "Believe me, my dear friend Crito, misstatements are not merely jarring in their immediate context; they also have a bad effect upon the soul. No, you must keep up your spirits and say that it is only my body that you are burying, and you can bury it as you please, in whatever way you think is most proper" (115e-116a).[56]

This farewell address has demonstrated unity in its use of apparently disparate traditional material. It unified such diverse sayings as predictions of Jesus' last passover, the Eucharist, warnings of betrayal, a dispute over greatness and teaching on authority, commissioning of the twelve apostles with a special role for Simon, and the warning about changing circumstances of their ministry. It highlighted the poignancy of the last supper narrative. In his parting meal, Jesus gave his disciples the Eucharist to bring the sacramental presence of his saving death to future generations. He prepared them for the shock of their betraying and failing him and foretold their eventual repentance and restoration to favor. He corrected their misunderstandings about authority and gave them au-

---

[55]Tannehill, *Narrative Unity*, 267, suggests that the transgressors among whom Jesus was numbered were the apostles, who transgressed by using the sword at Jesus' arrest (Lk 22: 49-51). By rebuking them and healing the man they wounded, Jesus shows his disapproval of their action, even though it seemed to flow from his previous directives about having swords. They transgressed by trusting in the sword and not in God. This explanation seems labored, but the others also fail to be self-evident.

[56]E. Hamilton and H. Cairns, eds., *The Collected Dialogues of Plato including the Letters* (Bollingen Series LXXI; Princeton, NJ: Princeton Univ., 1961) 95-96.

thority over the restored Israel. He prophesied Simon's denial but put him over all the apostles. He warned them that they will face more hostility in their mission than they have previously. Since they were unable to understand him until after the resurrection and Pentecost, Jesus ended the dialogue facing his death alone.

For contemporary Christianity, the insights that the farewell setting sheds on the meaning of the Eucharist, of Christian authority and of apostolic ordination are the most important. The farewell setting recalls the sacrificial dimensions of the Eucharist as a counterweight to overemphasis on Eucharist as community meal. The farewell also emphasizes Jesus' lesson that Christian authority is not for self-aggrandizement or power but to serve the Church. The commission of the twelve apostles at this first Eucharist also restores attention to the indispensible role of ordained ministers of the Eucharist at a time when some churches are experiencing their shortage.

3

John 13-14

Explicit farewell elements dominate the five chapters of John 13-17, but the length of this section, the repetitiveness in its themes, and its apparently later additions distract from its clarity as a unified farewell address. This chapter shall focus on John 13-17 precisely as a farewell address, though in its present form it is probably *composite*.[57] Despite their composite nature, these chapters have more of the dynamics of a speech than Luke 22 and most synoptic speeches, which string together several shorter traditional sayings. Unlike most NT speeches which are monologues, this begins as a dialogue (Jn 13-14), but after its apparently original ending (14:31), the rest intersperses monologue (Jn 15:1-16:15 and the prayers in Jn 17) with dialogue (Jn 16:16-33). These chapters result in a much longer speech than Luke 22. Of the other NT farewell addresses, only Acts 20 is clearly a speech as distinguished from a collection of sayings made to look like a speech. But Acts 20 is a short speech written for the narrative, much like the other speeches in Acts and in Hellenistic historiography. It is more a synopsis than an actual speech, which would have far more repetition and detail.[58] In this respect, John 13-17 has more the dynamics of an actual farewell speech than Acts 20. Because of its repetitions and apparent additions, John 13-17 does not have the tight structure that makes for easy analysis

---

[57]See R. Alter, *The Art of Biblical Narrative* (New York: Basic Books, 1981) ch 7, "Composite Artistry," 131-54; Sternberg, *Poetics*, "Source and Discourse," 13-23.

[58]Cf. G. H. R. Horsley, "Speeches and Dialogue in Acts," *NTS* 32 (1986) 609-14 on the unreal brevity of the Acts speeches.

as do Luke 22 and Acts 20. This chapter will intersperse paragraph by paragraph analysis with concentrated study of individual themes that are scattered throughout these chapters, such as Jesus' departure, his promise of the Paraclete, and unity among believers.

The narrator establishes the farewell setting at the beginning of chapter 13. "Now before the feast of the Passover, when Jesus knew that his hour had come to depart out of this world to the Father, having loved his own who were in the world, he loved them to the end" (Jn 13:1). The mention of Jesus' imminent departure and love of his own "to the end" provides the setting not only for the footwashing in chapter 13, but for all the speech material in John 13-17 until the shift to the garden where Judas betrayed him (Jn 18:1).[59]

Jesus washes his disciples' feet to express his love for them "to the end," knowing his hour has come to leave this world for the Father. The devil has already provided the tragic background for Jesus' washing of their feet by putting it into Judas' heart to betray him (Jn 13:2). The narrator also mentions Jesus' sense of determining his own destiny, having come from God and about to return to God. His act of stripping and of washing his disciples' feet shows his love for his disciples, including his betrayer, and signals his return to his Father from this world.

Readers through the ages have tended to identify with Peter's shocked reaction: "Lord, do you wash my feet?" (Jn 13:6). Jesus' answer, which Peter understands later, fails to convince him then. Only Jesus' threat that Peter's refusal would separate him from Jesus persuades Peter to let Jesus wash his

---

[59]The apparent change in place signaled by "Rise, let us go hence," at the end of John 14 provides a break which does not seem accounted for in John 15-17, where Jesus seems to continue the conversation from chapter 14. Historical critics have generally explained this as a seam between two sources: cf. Schnackenburg, *St. John* 1.46, 73, 3.87-90; Brown, *John XIII-XXI*, 2.582-88. But narrative criticism reads John 13-17 as a single composite narrative, even if historically it combines multiple sources. Read as a unit with John 13-14, the further discourse in John 15-17 seems either to delay response to Jesus' invitation to leave, or the readers are to imagine the further discourse taking place on the way to the garden mentioned in John 18:1. The statement at the end of the whole discourse, that Jesus went out with his disciples after speaking these words (Jn 18:1), makes the delay approach more plausible.

feet. Jesus then indicates that he knew even when he washed Judas' feet that Judas would betray him. The post-resurrection perspective helps clarify the relationship of Jesus' washing the feet of both friends and betrayer to his death on the cross for all humans. Jesus' symbolic act of footwashing places him in a self-effacing role doing what only a slave would do, just as only a slave or the lowest alien criminals were crucified. Both acts were meant to cleanse sinners through self sacrifice by the only Son of the Father.

The footwashing symbolically begins Jesus' departure to his Father. In this respect, it has the same function in the Johannine farewell address that the Eucharist has in the Lukan. Both symbolically express what will take place on the cross, and after performing each, Jesus asks his disciples to imitate his action. In Luke Jesus tells them to "do this in memory of me" (Lk 22:19). In John he says, "Do you know what I have done to you?... If I then, your Lord and Teacher, have washed your feet, you also ought to wash one another's feet. For I have given you an example (*hypodeigma*), that you also should do as I have done to you" (Jn 13:14-15).

However, the kind of Christian imitation of the Lukan Eucharist and Johannine footwashing seems to have been different. The fact that Luke's version of the Eucharist departs from his usual source, Mark, to follow Paul's version, apparently because that was the version currently in liturgical use in the churches with which he was most familiar, gives more evidence for the Eucharist's being sacramentally reenacted in the Christian churches than there is for John's footwashing. As Fitzmyer says, Luke is clearly trying to root the Christian celebration of the "Lord's Supper" in his account of the Last Supper.[60]

Jesus' knowledge of his betrayer makes his footwashing an even more striking example for his disciples to imitate. They are to humble themselves in service to others, even to those who may be unworthy. Jesus underscores his command that they imitate his action by reminding them that they, the ser-

[60]For a discussion of the Christian liturgical origins and intentions behind Luke's account, with bibliography, see Fitzmyer, 2.1393-1405.

vants, are not greater than he, the master (Jn 13:16), and cannot expect to be spared doing what their master has done. "If you know these things, blessed are you if you do them" (v 17).

Jesus immediately follows this act and instruction by foretelling his betrayal by one of them. Such farewell warnings prepare followers for reversals and forestall the scandal they might otherwise cause. Later unbelievers were to ask why Jesus had selected a traitor for his inner circle. The speech explicitly answers this objection: "I know whom I have chosen; it is that the scripture may be fulfilled, 'He who ate my bread has lifted his heel against me.' I tell you this now, before it takes place, that when it does take place you may believe that I am he" (vv 18-19). As in so many Johannine passages, Jesus seems to be speaking directly to the later Christian community, the implied readers. His statements directly address their concerns.

During the disciples' reaction to Jesus' betrayal prophecy, the narrator first introduces the "beloved disciple" (Jn 13:23). The historical implication of his leaving him unnamed is that the intended readers already knew his identity. The literary implication of the narrator's waiting till Jesus' farewell address before first introducing an important, familiar character seems to be that that character is more important for the time of the readers than for the public life of Jesus. The narrator introduces the beloved disciple as a contrast to the traitor, Judas, and as closer to Jesus than the obvious leader among the disciples, Peter. Only later will the narrative fill the gap for the readers caused by this delayed mention of an unnamed but known disciple.[60a]

[60a]On the beloved disciple, cf. esp. Schnackenburg, *St. John* 3. 375-88, bibliographical notes 3.484-86; Brown, *John I-XII*, pp xcii-xcviii, with changed view in *John XIII-XXI*, 922-27, 1004-08, 1081-82, 1122-25; R. E. Brown, *The Community of the Beloved Disciple* (New York: Paulist, 1979) 31-34; M. Passment, "The Fourth Gospel's Beloved Disciple," *ExpTim* 94/12 (1982-83) 363-67, p 366 discusses named and unnamed characters in John; D.J. Hawkin, "The Function of the Beloved Disciple Motif in the Johannine Redaction," *LTP* 33 (1977) 135-50; P. Minear, "The Beloved Disciple in the Gospel of John," *NovT* 19 (1977) 105-23; B. Byrne, "The Faith of the Beloved Disciple and the Community in John 20," *JSNT* 23 (1985) 83-97; W. Kurz, "The Beloved Disciple and Implied Readers," *BTB* 19/3 (July 1989) 100-07.

The crucifixion scene confirms the beloved disciple's importance for this community of readers after Jesus' death. Just before he dies, Jesus gives his mother (never named in John), whom he calls "Woman," to the beloved disciple, and the beloved disciple to his mother (Jn 19:25-27).

> When Jesus saw his mother, and the disciple whom he loved standing near, he said to his mother, "Woman, behold, your son!" Then he said to the disciple, "Behold, your mother!" And from that hour the disciple took her to his own home (Jn 19:26-27).

At Cana before his "hour had come" his mother (also called "Woman" there) had told the servants, "Do whatever he tells you" (Jn 2:1-5).

> On the third day there was a marriage at Cana in Galilee, and the mother of Jesus was there; Jesus also was invited to the marriage, with his disciples. When the wine gave out, the mother of Jesus said to him, "They have no wine." And Jesus said to her, "O woman, what have you to do with me? My hour has not yet come." His mother said to the servants, "Do whatever he tells you." (Jn 2:1-5).

The narrator is clearly linking the two passages by this odd use of "Woman" and "mother" in the context of Jesus' hour.[61]

Withholding the name of the mother or woman in both places not only suggests that the implied readers knew her identity, it also allows the narrator to use "woman" and "mother" symbolically.[62] At both Cana and the cross, the mother refers to the historical Mary but also alludes to the Church, mother of Christians, who tells people to "Do whatever he tells you," and to whom the beloved disciple is entrusted (cf. a similar overlap between mother of Jesus and Church in Rev 12). Withholding the name of the beloved disciple also

---

[61]Cf. J. A. Grassi, "The Role of Jesus' Mother in John's Gospel," *CBQ* 48 (1986) 67-80.

[62]Cf. Minear, "Beloved Disciple," 105- 06.

enables the narrator to use him not only for that historical individual whom chapter 21 identifies as the source of the Gospel (Jn 21:24), but also to suggest all disciples of Jesus, "whom he loves." Jesus' entrusting the Church to the beloved disciple at the cross could well refer to the historical leadership of the Johannine community by that beloved disciple. But it could also suggest that Jesus on the cross gave the Church as mother to all his beloved disciples, to all readers of John's Gospel.[63]

The beloved disciple, who was probably both the source of the Gospel (Jn 21:24) and the founder of the community of the implied readers, found out from Jesus who the betrayer would be (Jn 13:25-26), but that did not affect the outcome. When Judas ate the telltale morsel, Satan entered into him and Jesus immediately dismissed him to do his deed (v 27). The imagery is quite ominous: Satan entered Judas, Judas went out, "and it was night" (vv 27, 30). The reference to night recalls the extensive Johannine imagery of darkness opposing light (Jn 1:5; 3:19; 8:12; 12:35-36, 46) and being under Satan "the ruler of this world" (cf. Jn 12:31). Jesus is the light of the world, but Judas, like many, prefers the darkness to the light (Jn 3:19). He walks in the darkness under Satan's power. Through dramatic irony Judas' betrayal becomes a model for sin and choice of darkness over light, as Jesus' footwashing becomes a model for true discipleship.

With the departure of Judas the Gospel theme of the glorification of Jesus approaches its climax (v 31). The narrator had introduced the theme with his aside to the readers in John 7:39: "Now this he said about the Spirit, which those who believed in him were to receive; for as yet the Spirit had not been given, because Jesus was not yet glorified." The theme of glorification is further developed in Jesus' debate with the Jews in chapter 8, when he claims that he is not glorifying himself, but God is glorifying him (Jn 8:54). Jesus' remark that Lazarus' death will lead to the glorification of the Son (Jn

---

[63]See esp. Byrne, "Disciple and Community," 93-94 on the beloved disciple as the point of insertion for later generations into pivotal events of the Gospel; cf. Hawkin, "Function," 136, 138, esp. n 15 with bibliography.

11:4) continues the theme. Another aside by the narrator refers to Jesus' glorification: "His disciples did not understand this at first; but when Jesus was glorified, then they remembered that this had been written of him and had been done to him" (Jn 12:16). Jesus refers to his impending glorification in the same chapter 12: "The hour has come for the Son of man to be glorified" (v 23). In the Johannine equivalent of the agony in the garden in the synoptic Gospels Jesus says he will not ask the Father to save him from this hour but to glorify his name, and the heavenly voice responds, "I have glorified it, and I will glorify it again" (12:28). Jesus refers to the judgment of this world, "and I, when I am lifted up from the earth, will draw all to myself" (12:32). This closely related image of being lifted up goes back to chapter 3: "And as Moses lifted up the serpent in the wilderness, so must the Son of man be lifted up, that whoever believes in him may have eternal life" (Jn 3:14-15). It is echoed in Jesus' debate with the Jews in chapter 8: "When you have lifted up the Son of man, then you will know that I am he" (Jn 8:28). Both these themes come to their climax in John 13:31-32: "Now is the Son of man glorified, and in him God is glorified; if God is glorified in him, God will also glorify him in himself, and glorify him at once." Being glorified and "lifted up" are Johannine ironic puns that allude both to Jesus' ignominious crucifixion and to his exaltation to God through his crucifixion. Jesus' moment of glorification has finally arrived.

Therefore he again says goodbye to his disciples, telling them that he is only to be with them a little while, and that they cannot follow him where he goes (Jn 13:33). As he leaves them, he gives them a new commandment, that they love one another as he has loved them. Their love for each other will be the sign by which others will know they are his disciples (vv 34-35). Jesus answers Peter's question about where he is going by telling him he cannot follow him now, but shall do so later (v 36). Peter understands the reference to death and protests he is willing to follow Jesus now to death. But Jesus retorts that instead Peter will deny him three times (vv 37-38). The farewell elements are prominent and poignant. The long-awaited glorification of Jesus is about to take place. The disciples will not be able to follow Jesus to death at present, though they will in the future. In the meantime, he gives them his final and new commandment to love one another as the sign by which they will be recognized as his followers.

There is no break between chapters. Jesus reassures his disciples (Jn 14:1) immediately after predicting Peter's triple denial (13:38). "Let not your hearts be troubled; believe in God, believe also in me" (14:1). This section of the farewell address is a dialogue that focuses on reassurance to the disciples: Jesus goes ahead (beyond death) to prepare a place for them; he is the way to the Father. What believers ask in his name he will do; he will give them the Spirit as their Paraclete. He gives them his lasting peace and urges them to rejoice that he is going to the Father.

Jesus first reassures his disciples that he goes to prepare a place for them in his Father's house.

> In my Father's house are many rooms; if it were not so, would I have told you that I go to prepare a place for you? And when I go and prepare a place for you, I will come again and will take you to myself, that where I am you may be also (Jn 14:2-4).

Although Jesus is clearly leaving them and passing through the gates of death, he will return and bring his disciples to him in his Father's house after their deaths. The reference to Jesus' returning is ambiguous: many parts of the NT give evidence of intense apocalyptic expectation that Jesus would soon return bringing on the final judgment at the end of the world, but John's Gospel tends to speak more often of the end of each person's world in death and the judgment already effected when one chooses for or against Jesus. Here the Johannine form of personal eschatology at death seems the more likely referent.

The dialogue next reassures the disciples (and readers) that Jesus is the way to the Father.

> "And you know the way where I am going." Thomas said to him, "Lord, we do not know where you are going; how can we know the way?" Jesus said to him, "I am the way, and the truth, and the life; no one comes to the Father, but by me" (Jn 14:4-6).

The dialogue uses a character's ignorance and misunderstanding to make its point, as it so often does in the Fourth Gospel (e.g., Nicodemus in Jn 3). The narrator had first mentioned Thomas in chapter 11 as perceiving their risk in going to Lazarus: "Thomas, called the Twin, said to his fellow disciples, 'Let us also go, that we may die with him'" (Jn 11:16). This same Thomas will later refuse to believe the other disciples' witness that Jesus has risen, thus providing the occasion for a physical demonstration of Jesus' resurrection (hand in his side) and for the most exalted christological confession in the Gospel, "My Lord and my God!" (Jn 20:24-28). In this passage Thomas expresses the lack of understanding that gives Jesus the occasion to emphasize, "I am the way, and the truth, and the life; no one comes to the Father, but by me" (Jn 14:6). This bold statement encouraged beleaguered believers by directly challenging the Jewish synagogues from which the Johannine community had recently been expelled (cf. Jn 9:22, "for the Jews had already agreed that if any one should confess him to be Christ, he was to be put out of the synagogue"; 12:42; 16:2, "They will put you out of the synagogues"). Despite the unbelief by many in Jesus, he is the only way to the Father. Those who refuse to accept Jesus, such as those who historically rejected him in his lifetime and in the preaching of the Johannine Church, will not be able to reach the Father. The boldness of the statement was reassuring to the Johannine Christians that they were on the right track, even if the majority of people ("the world" around them) rejected it.

The statement (and the many like it in the Fourth Gospel) provides an even greater challenge to a contemporary mindset that relativizes religions. Ecumenism and interfaith dialogue cannot depend upon a relinquishing of the basis of one's faith, and the belief that Jesus is the only mediator to the Father is the cornerstone of the Christian faith. Members of other religions may not like it, but this is what Christians believe and what they must bring to any dialogue. Christians do not like the Jewish denial that Jesus is God or Messiah any more than Jews like their Christian affirmation. Nor would either Christians or Jews appreciate a Hindu reduction of Jesus to just one of countless incarnations of God. But they must expect to hear this from Hindus. So should other religions expect to hear Christians profess their faith in Christ. Professing Christian belief in Christ need not imply belligerence toward other religions, even though competing claims of different religions cannot always be mutually reconciled. The Church in Vatican II affirmed that other religions help people to reach God, so its insistence that Jesus is the only mediator to the Father is by no means a condemnation of all other religions.[64] In the NT view, which has been reasserted in Pope John Paul II's recent encyclical, *Redemptor Hominis*, Jesus has reconciled all fallen humans to God. It is only because of this reconciliation that *any* people of any religious background can and do reach God.[65]

The farewell dialogue turns next to Jesus' identification with the Father and their mutual indwelling:

> "If you had known me, you would have known my Father also; henceforth you know him and have seen him." Philip said to him, "Lord, show us the Father, and we shall be satisfied." Jesus said to him, "Have I been with you so long, and yet you do not know me, Philip? He who has seen me has seen the Father; how can you say, 'Show us the Father'? Do you not believe that I am in the Father and the Father in me? The words that I say to you I do not speak on my own authority; but the Father who dwells in me does his works. Believe me that I am in the Father and the Father in me; or else believe me for the sake of the works themselves" (Jn 14:7-11).

The step from Jesus as the mediating way to the Father to the mutual indwelling of Father and Son is not a difficult one for the exalted christology of the Fourth Gospel (e.g., Jn 8:28-29, "he who sent me is with me; he has not left me alone"; 8:58, "before Abraham was, I am"; 10:38, "believe the works, that

[64]See the Vatican II Declaration on the Relation of the Church to Non-Christian Religions, *Nostra aetate*.

[65]Pope John Paul II, "The Redeemer of Man" (*Redemptor Hominis*. Boston: St. Paul Editions, 1979).

you may know and understand that the Father is in me and I am in the Father"). The narrator places this christological statement within the poignant farewell setting of Jesus' long-time association with the disciples and imminent departure.

After Andrew, the other follower of the Baptist (Jn 1:35-42), and Simon Peter, Philip was the first disciple whom Jesus called in John's Gospel. Philip in turn brought Nathanael to Jesus (Jn 1:43-48). At the multiplication of the loaves, it was Philip whom Jesus tested by asking how they would feed the multitude, after which Andrew reported about the boy with the five loaves and two fish (Jn 6:5-9). When some Greeks wanted to see Jesus, they came first to Philip, who with Andrew interceded for them (Jn 12:20-22). Jesus' plaint, "Have I been with you so long, and yet you do not know me, Philip?" has pathos reinforced by all these previous experiences. Jesus' answer to him about the mutual indwelling of Father and Son recalls the many images in the Fourth Gospel of Jesus as Word that reveals the Father: for example, "No one has ever seen God; the only Son, who is in the bosom of the Father, he has made him known" (Jn 1:18).

Jesus' mention of his works in 14:11, "or else believe me for the sake of the works themselves," leads into his next statement:

> Truly, truly, I say to you, he who believes in me will also do the works that I do; and greater works than these will he do, because I go to the Father. Whatever you ask in my name, I will do it, that the Father may be glorified in the Son; if you ask anything in my name, I will do it (Jn 14:12-14).

These promises fit the farewell genre as promises and provision for the future of one's disciples after one's departure. Jesus promises that his disciples will do greater works than he *because* he goes to the Father. It is possible to understand among the "greater works" the worldwide expansion of the Church. Jesus' departure to the Father through death and resurrection will be the source of power for his disciples both to emulate his own (miraculous) works, and to spread the good news throughout the world. Likewise, Jesus promises that he will do whatever they ask in his name.

The recent resurgence of healings and charismatic gifts in the mainline churches has illustrated the enduring validity for the Church even today of the signs and wonders included in Christ's promise that believers "will also do the works that I do." The Acts of the Apostles had portrayed the early fulfillment of Christ's promises by showing his followers spreading the gospel and working the same kinds of miracles he had worked. Through the ages, saints have continued to work similar miracles in Jesus' name. Pilgrimage sites and shrines have for centuries been the locus of many healings. The past twenty years have seen a kind of "democratization" of such healings in the Catholic Church as many ordinary people have been involved in praying for and experiencing healings that go beyond medical explanation. As priests and people approach the Sacrament of the Sick with greater expectancy, many sick are healed. Healing services are common in many parishes. More and more parents are praying over their sick children, many prayer groups lay hands on and pray over the sick, and many are cured. Our contemporary experience confirms Jesus' promise that we would continue to perform the works he did.

A major element both for the farewell genre and for the theology of John 13-17 is Jesus' promise of a Paraclete or Counselor to be with Christians after his departure. The speech interweaves the promise of the Paraclete throughout several chapters (Jn 14:15-17, 25-26; 15:26; 16:7-15), but for clarity's sake the references will be discussed together here.[66] The Paraclete passages emphasize the following points: though the disciples will receive the Holy Spirit, the world will not; after Jesus' departure the Paraclete will continue to enlighten his disciples, recall his teachings and bear witness to him; the Paraclete will convict the world that they sinned in rejecting Jesus, and that God has vindicated Jesus and has judged Satan, the world's ruler. The passages specify that the revelation which the Paraclete brings is not new but a recollection of the same revelation Jesus brought.

[66]See esp. Brown, *John XIII-XXI* 1135-44; Brown, *Community*, 138-44; Schnackenburg, *St. John*, 3.138-54, with bibliographical notes 427-30; R. Kysar, *The Fourth Evangelist and His Gospel* (Minneapolis: Augsburg, 1975) 234-40.

The Paraclete first appears in John's Gospel in the farewell as a parting gift from Jesus to his disciples.

> If you love me, you will keep my commandments. And I will pray the Father, and he will give you another Counselor, to be with you for ever, even the Spirit of truth, whom the world cannot receive, because it neither sees him nor knows him; you know him, for he dwells with you, and will be in you (Jn 14:15-17).

Jesus refers to him as "another Counselor" (or Paraclete) besides himself whose role after his departure is to do what Jesus did for the disciples. The phrase "another Paraclete" implies that Jesus himself is a Paraclete. The First Letter of John gives evidence that the Johannine community did apply the term Paraclete to Jesus himself: "but if anyone does sin, we have an advocate [or Paraclete] with the Father, Jesus Christ the righteous" (1 Jn 2:1). However, First John's use of Paraclete for Jesus is not the same as the Gospel's uses of that term for the Holy Spirit: in First John the risen Jesus acts as a defense attorney in heaven before God's judgment seat on behalf of sinners. In the Gospel the "other Paraclete," the Holy Spirit, has a different function, the advisory role of guiding Christians toward the truth in this life.

In John's Gospel Jesus himself is the truth and speaks it. "I am the way, and the truth, and the life; no one comes to the Father, but by me" (Jn 14:6). In the climax of his defense before Pilate, he declares, "For this I was born, and for this I have come into the world, to bear witness to the truth. Every one who is of the truth hears my voice" (18:37). Since Jesus is the truth, it is natural to refer to the "other Paraclete" as the Spirit of truth: "he will guide you into all the truth" (16:13). In the later Johannine theological setting 1 John contrasts the Spirit of truth in the disciples with the spirit of error in the world:

> They are of the world, therefore what they say is of the world, and the world listens to them. We are of God. Whoever knows God listens to us, and he who is not of God does not listen to us. By this we know the spirit of truth and the spirit of error (1 Jn 4:5-6).

The Johannine emphasis on truth can sound alien to minds raised on values clarification and religious and philosophical pluralism. It is totally foreign to relativism.[67] It is therefore not surprising that John's Gospel itself is labeled "sectarian" and its current relevance dismissed.[68] It is simply too alien to the contemporary Western mentality.

Since I believe that John's Gospel is the inspired word of God, I tend to regard such a clash between its values and those of contemporary culture more as a judgment on the culture than on the Gospel. The Fourth Gospel challenges our cultural *a prioris* in a way necessary to our mental health. According to a famous saying of Socrates, "The unexamined life is not worth living." The unexamined relativism of many Americans is deadly, not only for religion but for moral decency and the common good. I welcome the Fourth Gospel's challenges to some of the most basic unexamined presuppositions in our time. Its potentiality for sectarianism is balanced by other books of the canon. In the context of canon and Church tradition its insistence on truth is an indispensable part of the biblical revelation, especially for our culture.

Since the world rejected Jesus, it cannot receive the other Paraclete. He is a special gift to the disciples because they accepted Jesus. Reception of the Holy Spirit requires a choice to accept Jesus as teacher, guide and master of one's life. "If you love me, you will keep my commandments. And I will pray the Father and he will give you another Counselor...." (Jn 14:15-16). Jesus cannot trust the power of his Holy Spirit to those who will not obey and submit their lives to him. Divine power can only be exercised appropriately by those living in submission to the divine will. Only disciples who obey Jesus enjoy intimacy with him, and only those can receive his Holy Spirit. As Jesus had dwelt with the disciples but not with the world, so shall the Holy Spirit dwell with and in them alone.

[67]Cf. A. Bloom, *The Closing of the American Mind* (New York: Simon and Schuster, 1987) 25-26.

[68]A classic introduction to sectarian dimensions of the Fourth Gospel is W. A. Meeks, "The Man from Heaven in Johannine Sectarianism," *JBL* 91 (1972) 44-72.

The Spirit shall be with the Church through every age, "forever" (Jn 14:16). The Church shall never be without the Paraclete's guidance. The time of the apostles is not to be some golden age after which the Church is to go through silver, bronze and iron ages of decline from its pristine fervor. The Spirit will always live within the Church to give it divine life and keep it from error. Christians do not have to rely only on Scripture, since the same living Spirit of truth which produced the Scripture continues to live in the Church and in them, its members. This is why the Holy Spirit, the other Paraclete, is the most significant farewell gift of Jesus in the Fourth Gospel.

The Paraclete continues Jesus' teaching functions and bears witness to Jesus (14:25-26; 15:26).

> These things I have spoken to you, while I am still with you. But the Counselor, the Holy Spirit, whom the Father will send in my name, he will teach you all things, and bring to your remembrance all that I have said to you (Jn 14:25-26).

> But when the Counselor comes, whom I shall send to you from the Father, even the Spirit of truth, who proceeds from the Father, he will bear witness to me (Jn 15:26).

The Paraclete continues to guide the Church in "all things, and [will] bring to your remembrance all that I [Jesus] have said to you" (14:26). This promise is made originally to the assembled leaders of the Church, not to isolated Christians. It uses the second person plural, not singular. It therefore cannot be used to promote an individualist mentality that says "I have the Bible and the Holy Spirit, I do not need a Church." Although he does speak to individuals who prayerfully read their Scripture, the Spirit is not given to teach and recall the gospel to individuals who choose isolation from other Christians. The Holy Spirit bears witness within Christians to the reality of Jesus and the truth of his words as they read the Scripture or pray or recall what he did or said. This internal witness of the Holy Spirit within Christians produces conviction about Christ that can withstand the world's unbelief, ridicule and persecution.

There is a natural tension between current teaching by the Spirit in the Church and ancient traditions enshrining Jesus' teaching. Overemphasis on the revelatory functions of the Paraclete could lead to new and deviant teachings in the later Church, as in fact it did in the Montanist crisis in the mid-second century. The Montanist emphasis on new revelations by the Holy Spirit apparently led some to claim that the Holy Spirit was supplementing Christ's revelation and certainly challenged the authority of the Church's hierarchical guardians of tradition.[69] John 16 addresses this tension by anchoring the current action of the Spirit in the historical event of Jesus Christ. The teaching that the Paraclete brings the later Church is not new teaching but that of Jesus (16:7-15).

> Nevertheless I tell you the truth: it is to your advantage that I go away, for if I do not go away, the Counselor will not come to you; but if I go, I will send him to you. And when he comes, he will convict the world concerning sin and righteousness and judgment: concerning sin, because they do not believe in me; concerning righteousness, because I go to the Father, and you will see me no more; concerning judgment, because the ruler of this world is judged.

> I have yet many things to say to you, but you cannot bear them now. When the Spirit of truth comes, he will guide you into all the truth; for he will not speak on his own authority, but whatever he hears he will speak, and he will declare to you the things that are to come. He will glorify me, for he will take what is mine and declare it to you. All that the Father has is mine; therefore I said that he will take what is mine and declare it to you (16:7-15).

This statement balances both a traditional and a developmental role of the Spirit. The truth the Spirit speaks is not "on his own authority," that is, not independent of the revelation in Christ. Later Christians cannot claim to have received new

[69]See the balanced treatment by J. Pelikan, *The Christian Tradition*, Vol 1: *The Emergence of the Catholic Tradition (100-600)* (Chicago: Univ. of Chicago, 1971) 97-108.

revelation from the Holy Spirit that is in any way discontinuous from Christ's revelation. Thus claims of new revelation by cults like the Montanists are ruled out *a priori.*

Yet the Holy Spirit will develop and deepen Christians' understanding of Christ's revelation. The Fourth Gospel itself does this with traditions common to it and the synoptic Gospels, rendering explicit many truths about Christ's divinity that were mostly implicit in the Synoptics. Already in the writing of John's Gospel, the Holy Spirit "glorifies" Jesus by declaring "what is mine," including his unity with the Father and his divinity, "and declaring it to you." What the disciples were unable to bear before the resurrection, the Spirit of truth makes clear to the Church. "He will guide you into all the truth." He will guide the development of dogmatic understanding and later Christian insight into biblical truths. Though the revelation was definitive in the coming of the Word among flesh (Jn 1), the Church never stops learning its fuller implications or applications to times and circumstances.

Finally, the Holy Spirit "will declare to you the things that are to come" (Jn 16:13). Possibly, this is an allusion to Isaiah 44:7, "Who has announced from of old the things to come? Let them tell us what is yet to be"—which Isaiah uses as evidence for the true God. John 16:13 seems to refer to Christian prophecy of the future, including eschatological predictions.[70] This reference to prophecy is all the more striking in a Gospel which says so little about Christian prophecy in comparison to other NT documents like the Synoptics, Acts, Revelation, and quite a few of the letters. Though future prophecy is not a major theme in John's Gospel, the reference in verse 13 seems to show the minor influence on that Gospel of Christian tradition common to much of the NT.

The Paraclete's coming will affect not only Christians and their understanding of revelation, but also the unbelieving world. The first part of this passage relies heavily on legal imagery for the Holy Spirit's function *vis-à-vis* the world. When the Paraclete comes, he will convict the world in three ways. He will "prosecute" the world for not believing in Christ.

[70]B. Lindars, *The Gospel of John* (NCB; Grand Rapids: Eerdmans, 1972) 505.

He will vindicate Christ whom the world rejected but who is now with the Father. And he will judge the ruler of this world, Satan (cf. Jn 12:31, "now shall the ruler of this world be cast out"). The Holy Spirit will prove to Christians that the world is wrong and Jesus, whom the world rejects, is God's Son. The Holy Spirit will give Christians their conviction of truth and the courage to profess it before a hostile world.

Thus the Holy Spirit whom Jesus can only send if he goes to the Father (16:7) is Jesus' most signficant farewell gift to his followers. The Holy Spirit brings to completion the work begun in Christ's lifetime. The Spirit enables Christians to understand who Christ is and what his relationship is to the Father. The Spirit guides the Church into the future, protecting it from a hostile world. Jesus could have given his followers no greater gift than the Holy Spirit.

Closely related to the gift of the Spirit is Christ's farewell gift of peace to his followers. Immediately after promising that the Paraclete will bring to the their minds all that Jesus has taught them (Jn 14:26), Jesus bequeaths his peace to the disciples.

> Peace I leave with you; my peace I give to you; not as the world gives do I give to you. Let not your hearts be troubled, neither let them be afraid (Jn 14:27).

Christians through the ages have emphasized the importance of Christ's peace as a sign of the Holy Spirit's work and presence and as a sign of union with Christ and being in his will. The Johannine context of this promise is Jesus' impending suffering. Christ's peace is not Pollyanna avoidance of reality or escapism. It is not self-induced through oriental or other methods of physical and mental relaxation. Christ's peace is a gift, not something produced by human methods, effort or merit.

Jesus gives his peace to his disciples, to those who submit their lives fully to him and to his Father's will. The gift of peace follows the surrender of one's own desires to seek God's perfect will. Peace is not only "the tranquility of order," according to the classic Thomistic philosophical definition, but the tranquility of being in God's order, being where the Creator wants his creature to be. Christ's peace is not something purely passive, but requires the cooperative effort of submitting one's own will to the Father's. Jesus also wants the effort of refusing to give in to fear and anxiety: "Let not your hearts be troubled, neither let them be afraid" (Jn 14:27b). We can choose whether we will give in to anxiety or resist it. We can reject anxiety with our wills by refusing to dwell on our problems or delve into all their ramifications, and instead surrender all problems to Christ's power and submit ourselves to God's perfect will, asking him to guide us into whatever responses are appropriate. By refusing to focus on problems that cause anxiety, and by placing ourselves at the mercy of God's providence, we lay the groundwork for Christ's gift of peace. His peace is directly correlated to our trust in him to guide our lives and provide for our needs.

Christ does not give peace as the world does (Jn 14:27). The world's peace can be the result of human efforts, self-help techniques, oriental meditation methods, or simply the relief that comes after a decision (good or bad) ends a long struggle of conscience. This does not necessarily indicate that the person has Christ's peace or is in God's will. It may just be the relief that comes when one stops fighting interior battles of conscience and has no necessary correlation to whether or not the final choice was sinful. But if the choice was not God's will, Christ's peace will be lacking. Those who choose against God's will are "on their own," with the anxiety that naturally follows when later crises arise.

Nor can the world's peace be lasting, "for the form of this world is passing away" (1 Cor 7:31b). Everything temporal is also temporary and transitory. Peace based on any earthly arrangement or balance of forces must of its nature pass away. Success, riches, health, power, popularity and the like are all impermanent. So is any peace based on them. Even the more subtle forms of peace from mental techniques and meditation are from the world, not Christ's gift. Insofar as they depend on human will and effort, they are as transient as the human activity on which they are based. Even at their best, worldly forms of peace are cut short by death, after which the only important kind of peace will be the divine peace associated with the "eternal life" Christ came to give (Jn 10:28: "and I give them eternal life, and they shall never perish, and no one shall snatch them out of my hand"). Since worldly kinds of peace perish in death, "He who loves his life loses it, and he who hates his life in this world will keep it for eternal life" (Jn 12:25). Only the surrender to God of one's life, of all one's hopes, desires, and fears, in submission to God's perfect will for oneself, will open the way for Christ's lasting peace to enter.

St. Ignatius Loyola calls the surrender of all one's hopes, desires and fears "indifference to all created things." Lack of such indifference blocks the peace of Christ: "He who loves his life loses it. . . . " (Jn 12:25). In the "Principle and Foundation" of his *Spiritual Exercises,* St. Ignatius recalls that humans are created for God, and all other things on earth are created to help them to reach God. Therefore we are to use them insofar as they help to our end, and rid ourselves of them insofar as they hinder us from our end.

> For this it is necessary to make ourselves indifferent to all created things in all that is allowed to the choice of our free will and is not prohibited to it; . . . desiring and choosing only what is most conducive for us to the end for which we are created.[71]

Ignatian indifference is a way to "hate one's life in this world and keep it for eternal life" (cf. Jn 12:25). To surrender to God all one's deepest desires brings a psychological experience of "losing one's life." Someone who has fallen in love with another's spouse first experiences grief upon breaking off the relationship and surrendering to God's will for his or her life. But Christ's peace is unattainable without such a loss. Indifference is a self-denying form of abandonment to God's providence and will for one's life in all its details. "Not as the world gives do I give to you" (Jn 14:27a). Since it clings to nothing in

---

[71]D. L. Fleming, *The Spiritual Exercises of St. Ignatius: A Literal Translation and a Contemporary Reading* (Study Aids on Jesuit Topics, 7; St. Louis: Institute of Jesuit Sources, 1978) par. 23 of the literal E. Mullan translation, p 22.

this world, indifference need fear losing nothing in this world and thus removes all obstacles to Christ's peace.

Christ's peace overcomes all the tribulations we encounter in this world. Later in this composite farewell dialogue, Jesus returns to the subject of peace. He has just prophesied that all his disciples will be scattered and abandon him (Jn 16:32).

> I have said this to you, that in me you may have peace. In the world you have tribulation; but be off good cheer, I have overcome the world (Jn 16:33).

Christ's peace can exist in the midst of afflictions and sufferings. Jesus never promised to free us from all distress in this world; in fact, he predicted we would suffer many tribulations for his sake. However, he did promise his peace in whatever circumstances we find ourselves. When we experience afflictions from the world as Christians, Christ tells us to "be of good cheer, I have overcome the world" (Jn 16:33). Christ's peace is not a freedom from suffering; rather, it comes from his victory over suffering and death by his resurrection, through which he has "overcome the world."

Thus, in Jesus' farewell, he left his disciples his peace by which to endure and overcome their sufferings in this world. John's Gospel is too realistic to envisage a trouble-free life in this world. But it offers hope and peace in whatever tribulations the world can inflict on us. Christ leaves us his peace, not as the world gives peace, but to keep our hearts from fear in the midst of afflictions. Nothing can destroy Christ's peace, which is based on abandonment to him and his Father, for he has "overcome the world." Not even death, which destroys the world's peace, can affect the peace of Christ, for he has also overcome death and promises eternal life for those who follow after him. "My sheep hear my voice, and I know them, and they follow me; and I give them eternal life, and they shall never perish, and no one shall snatch them out of my hand" (Jn 10:27-28).

Jesus follows his promise of peace in John 14:27 with a final statement that he is going to the Father and an apparent end to the dialogue.

You have heard me say to you, "I go away and I will come to you." If you loved me, you would have rejoiced, because I go to the Father; for the Father is greater than I. And now I have told you before it takes place, so that when it does take place, you may believe. I will no longer talk much with you, for the ruler of this world is coming. He has no power over me; but I do as the Father has commanded me, so that the world may know that I love the Father. Rise, let us go hence (14:28-31).

This apparent ending to the farewell dialogue builds to an emotional climax. Jesus promises both that he will leave and that he will return to his disciples. He wishes their love for him were great enough to rejoice in the good he will experience by returning to the Father. He underlines how he has foretold his sufferings so his disciples could believe when he went to his death. He emphasizes the urgency and shortness of time before Satan arrives for Jesus. He assures them that despite appearances, this is not a victory for Satan over Jesus, but Jesus' own choice to obey his Father and thus show his love for him. He flatly denies that Satan has any power over him. To demonstrate his love for the Father, he calls his disciples to rise from supper and go with him to meet his fate.

4

John 15-17

Chapter 15 resumes the previous dialogue taking no notice of what appears to be its finish at the end of chapter 14, "Rise, let us go hence" (Jn 14:31b). Most commentators understand John 14:31b as the original end of Jesus' farewell address, followed immediately by John 18:1, "When Jesus had spoken these words, he went forth with his disciples across the Kidron valley...." The next three chapters, 15-17, seem like later insertions to the address.[72] Even if chapters 15-17 are additions, this analysis is based on all five chapters (13-17) in the composite form in which they now appear. From that composite perspective, the narrative in chapter 15 does not take up Jesus' hint of departure ("let us go hence"), but it resumes the dialogue as if Jesus put off leaving for the garden to finish giving more farewell instructions to his disciples in the supper room.

Jesus compares himself to the true vine, the Father to the vinedresser who tends the vine, and the disciples to the branches that live and bear fruit on the vine.

> I am the true vine, and my Father is the vinedresser. Every branch of mine that bears no fruit, he takes away, and every branch that does bear fruit he prunes, that it may bear more fruit. You are already made clean by the word which I have spoken to you. Abide in me, and I in you. As the branch cannot bear fruit by itself, unless it abides in the vine, neither can you, unless you abide in me. I am the vine, you are the branches. He who abides in me, and I in him, he it is that

[72]Cf. Brown, *John XIII-XXI*, 582-88; Schnackenburg, *St. John*, 1.46; 3.4, 89-91.

bears much fruit, for apart from me you can do nothing. If a man does not abide in me, he is cast forth as a branch and withers; and the branches are gathered, thrown into the fire and burned. If you abide in me, and my words abide in you, ask whatever you will, and it shall be done for you. By this my Father is glorified, that you bear much fruit, and so prove to be my disciples (Jn 15:1-8).

Jesus' comparison to a vine recalls OT comparisons of Israel to a vine which God planted and then uprooted or exposed to its natural enemies when it did not bear good grapes.

My beloved had a vineyard on a very fertile hill. He dug it and cleared it of stones, and planted it with choice vines; he built a watchtower in the midst of it, and hewed out a wine vat in it; and he looked for it to yield grapes, but it yielded wild grapes. And now ... judge I pray you, between me and my vineyard. What more was there to do for my vineyard that I have not done in it? When I looked for it to yield grapes, why did it yield wild grapes? And now I will tell you what I will do to my vineyard. I will remove its hedge, and it shall be devoured.... (Isa 5:1b-5. See also Jer 2:21, Ezek 17:1-10, 19:10-14, Ps 80:8-16).

Jesus as "true vine" contrasts with all the false vineyards and vines mentioned in the prophets and psalms. "Yet I planted you a choice vine, wholly of pure seed. How then have you turned degenerate and become a wild vine?" (Jer 2:21). Whereas the old vines did not live up to the expectations of God who planted and cared for them, the true vine—Jesus —will bring forth wine-producing grapes and bear good fruit for his Father the vinedresser (Jn 15:1). The OT vine parables had God rooting out the whole vine (sending Israel into exile) when it went bad: "But the vine was plucked up in fury, cast down to the ground" (Ezek 19:12). Jesus as true vine will never go bad or be uprooted, but if Christians who are his branches go bad and fail to produce fruit, they will be cut off by the Father. John 15 applies God's care for his vine in the OT parables to the Father as vinedresser lopping off bad branches and pruning good branches that they may bear more fruit (Jn

15:2). In the cases of both the OT and NT vines, God looks for fruit from them and removes what is unproductive. In the OT parables when the whole vine was unproductive it was destroyed, whereas in John 15 the true vine Jesus cannot go bad, so God will remove only its degenerate branches.

Although Jesus' vine parable begins with the same theme of God's judgment on unfruitful vines or branches as the OT vine parables, its emphasis quickly changes to the necessity of being cleansed (the RSV translates the same Greek word by "cleanse" or "prune" according to context) and remaining on the vine. "You are already made clean by the word which I have spoken to you" (Jn 15:3). Since Judas has already departed, there is no need for a disclaimer that not all are clean, as in John 13:10b-11: "and you are clean, but not every one of you. For he knew who was to betray him; that was why he said, 'You are not all clean.'" Even if the John 15 vine sayings were originally added to John 13-14, they have narrative consistency to Judas's previous departure in chapter 13. The disciples now present are all clean, whereas the departed Judas is a degenerate branch who will be cast into the fire to burn (compare Jn 15:6 with 13:30, "So, after receiving the morsel, he [Judas] immediately went out; and it was night").

Jesus underlines the importance of his disciples being branches of the true vine, expressing the closest possible union between them and him:

> Abide in me, and I in you. As the branch cannot bear fruit by itself, unless it abides in the vine, neither can you, unless you abide in me. I am the vine, you are the branches. He who abides in me, and I in him, he it is that bears much fruit, for apart from me you can do nothing (Jn 15:4-5).

With its stress on mutual indwelling or abiding, the vine image implies an exalted christology and an organic ecclesiology comparable to the Pauline analogy of the Body of Christ (1 Cor 6:15; 10:17; 12:12, 27; more fully in Col 1:18 and Eph 1:23 and *passim*). Colossians combines an organic image of ecclesiastical union with Christ and an exalted christology: "He is the head of the body, the church.... For in him all the fulness of God was pleased to dwell...." (Col 1:18-19, cf.

1:15-16, "He is the image of the invisible God . . . for in him all things were created. . . ."). Ephesians also develops this combination of organic ecclesiology and exalted christology: God "chose us in him before the foundation of the world. . . ." (Eph 1:4) "and has made him the head over all things for the church, which is his body, the fulness of him who fills all in all" (Eph 1:23). "Rather, . . . we are to grow up in every way into him who is the head, into Christ, from whom the whole body . . . when each part is working properly, makes bodily growth and upbuilds itself in love" (Eph 4:15-16).

These images are probably developments from the earlier comparisons in 1 Corinthians: "Do you not know that your bodies are members of Christ? Shall I therefore take the members of Christ and make them members of a prostitute?" (1 Cor 6:15). Paul moves from this moral application to a eucharistic one: "The bread which we break, is it not a participation in the body of Christ? . . . we who are many are one body, for we all partake of the one bread" (1 Cor 10:16-17). Paul uses the same body image to express the ecclesiological significance of the gifts of the Spirit: "For just as the body is one and has many members, and all the members of the body, though many, are one body, so it is with Christ. For by one Spirit we were all baptized into one body, Jews or Greeks. . . ." (1 Cor 12:12-13). "Now you are the body of Christ and individually members of it. And God has appointed in the church first apostles, second prophets, third teachers, then workers of miracles. . . ." (1 Cor 12:27-28). As the Johannine vine image connotes organic union between Christians and Christ, so does the image of the body of Christ in the Pauline tradition. Both images combine an organic ecclesiology with an exalted view of Christ as Image and Son of God present at creation and giver of the divine Spirit.

The organic relationship between Christ and Christians or Christ and the Church as head and body or vine and branches expresses total dependence of the latter on Christ. Both images preclude a purely institutional view of the Church. Being organically linked with Christ, the Church is more than a human institution. It somehow extends Christ in space and time, and lives totally from Christ's life. In its human and institutional aspects, the Church has observable sins among its members and weaknesses in the way it has been structured in different times and places.[73] But as part of Christ the Vine or as the Body of Christ, the Church shares in Christ's divine life, spiritual power, redemptive mission and infallible teaching.

As branches cannot live or bear fruit without the vine (Jn 15), so Church members cannot live or bear fruit apart from Christ in his Church. At the last supper, Jesus addressed this analogy to his gathered disciples, who received the Holy Spirit and became the core of his post-resurrection Church, not to isolated individuals. Apart from Jesus, we can do nothing; withered branches are good only for the fire. With all the emphasis on community and mutual love in the Johannine Gospel and letters, it is clear that the link between branches and vine presumes a Church setting: this link is not maintained by individualists who reject Church membership to relate solely to Jesus. The First Letter of John makes this point even of groups who departed from the main community: "They went out from us, but they were not of us; for if they had been of us, they would have continued with us; but they went out, that it might be plain that they all are not of us" (1 Jn 2:19). The farewell setting of the vine image in John 15 reinforces its relationship to the Church. Jesus told this parable to the disciples who were to carry on his work in his name, with the Holy Spirit he was to give them, after his departure to the Father. In other words, he told it to his Church.

The image of vine and branches metaphorically and vividly expresses our organic dependence on Christ for our very life and fruitfulness as Christians. But it does not explain in what this organic and vital link consists or how Christians abide in Christ. The Gospel and First Letter of John keep returning to what it means to abide in Christ, often from different angles, so that gradually a fuller picture emerges. John 5:38 began with a negative perspective: to those Jews who did not believe in him, Jesus said, "and you do not have his word abiding in you, for you do not believe him whom he has sent." John 6:56, which comments on the eucharistic meaning of the feeding of the 5,000, linked abiding with the Eucharist: "He who eats my

[73]Cf. Vatican II "Dogmatic Constitution on the Church" (*Lumen Gentium*) par. 48.

flesh and drinks my blood abides in me, and I in him" (Jn 6:56). In the farewell itself, Jesus had earlier said to Philip,

> Do you not believe that I am in the father and the Father in me? The words that I say to you I do not speak on my own authority; but the Father who dwells in me does his works. Believe me that I am in the Father and the Father in me; or else believe me for the sake of the works themselves (Jn 14:10-11).

Jesus describes the Father's and his mutual indwelling with the same terms he used for the way he mutually abides with his disciples in the Eucharist and as the Vine. The three cases have the closest possible reciprocal presence and interpenetration. Slightly later, Jesus speaks the same way about Christians and the Holy Spirit: "you know him, for he dwells with you, and will be in you" (Jn 14:17). All these expressions describe a spiritual indwelling, even the initial negative example of God's word not abiding in those who disbelieve in Jesus. Coming earlier in John's Gospel, they prepare for the sustained emphasis on the mutual abiding of the Vine and branches in John 15. All forms of mutual abiding imply shared divine life, as between Father and Son, between Christ and his disciples in the Eucharist, and between the divine Spirit and the disciples.

The concerted teaching on mutual abiding in John 15 begins with Jesus' command to abide in him:

> Abide in me, and I in you. As the branch cannot bear fruit by itself, unless it abides in the vine, neither can you, unless you abide in me. I am the vine, you are the branches. He who abides in me, and I in him, he it is that bears much fruit, for apart from me you can do nothing (Jn 15:4-5).

One must make a choice: either to abide in Christ or to "go it alone" apart from Christ. The Greek term for "abide" also means "remain" and connotes perseverance and permanence in the relationship with Christ. Earlier the Gospel had depicted Jesus' sorrow when disciples stopped following him.

> Jesus said to the twelve, "Do you also wish to go away?"

Simon Peter answered him, "Lord, to whom shall we go? You have the words of eternal life; and we have believed, and have come to know, that you are the Holy One of God." Jesus answered them, "Did I not choose you, the twelve, and one of you is a devil?" He spoke of Judas the son of Simon Iscariot, for he, one of the twelve, was to betray him (Jn 6:67-71).

The First Letter of John expresses similar dismay when some do not persevere in the group's unity, as noted above: "They went out from us, but they were not of us; for if they had been of us, they would have continued with us; but they went out, that it might be plain that they all are not of us" (1 Jn 2:19). The theme of remaining in Christ is a primary concern throughout the Gospel and letters.

The vine image shows one of the reasons for this concern. "If a man does not abide in me, he is cast forth as a branch and withers; and the branches are gathered, thrown into the fire and burned" (Jn 15:6). John's Gospel emphasizes judgment for those who depart from Jesus or reject him initially. "He who believes in him [the Son] is not condemned; he who does not believe is condemned already, because he has not believed in the name of the only Son of God" (Jn 3:18). The First Letter of John applies the Gospel's judgment theme to perseverance of Christians: "And now, little children, abide in him, so that when he appears we may have confidence and not shrink from him in shame at his coming" (1 Jn 2:28). Judgment in John involves a separation in this life between the world and those who abide in Christ, but the reference in 1 John 2:28 to the appearance of Christ also refers to the final judgment after this life. Although the Johannine Gospel and letters do not mention hell by name, the statement that "the branches are gathered, thrown into the fire and burned" (Jn 15:6) must have carried allusions to eternal judgment and hell for any Christian readers. I think it improbable that the Johannine Christians were totally unaware of the many striking sayings of Jesus about hell, such as,

> And if your hand causes you to sin, cut it off; it is better for you to enter life maimed than with two hands to go to hell,

> to the unquenchable fire . . . it is better for you to enter the kingdom of God with one eye than with two eyes to be thrown into hell, where their worm does not die, and the fire is not quenched (Mk 9:43-48, par Mt 18:8-9).

In urging his disciples to abide in him, Jesus promises eternal life and love, which balances his reference to the judgment of those who do not abide in him.

> If you abide in me, and my words abide in you, ask whatever you will, and it shall be done for you. By this my Father is glorified, that you bear much fruit, and so prove to be my disciples. As the Father has loved me, so I have loved you; abide in my love. If you keep my commandments, you will abide in my love, just as I kept my Father's commandments and abide in his love. These things I have spoken to you, that my joy may be in you, and that your joy may be full (Jn 15:7-11).

Many blessings result from abiding in Jesus: answered prayer, fruitful evangelism, God's glory, abiding in his love, and complete joy. By remaining in Jesus when they petition the Father, Christians stand before the Father with the righteousness of Christ, not their own sinfulness.

The Father sees and responds to Christ, and therefore answers their prayers. For Christians to remain in Christ, they must retain his words within them. That is, they must assimilate and make their own the teachings of Jesus, or, in Pauline terms, "Have this mind among yourselves, which is yours in Christ Jesus" (Phil 2:5). A literal but highly effective way to have Christ's words abide in oneself is to meditate in the morning on a Gospel saying of Jesus (as in the Sermon on the Mount), asking God to reveal its meaning for one's own life, and then throughout the day to recall this saying, especially in one's problems and trials. For example, recalling Christ's words, "Blessed are the gentle," can dissipate one's anger when challenged, and lead to a response that is quiet and persuasive rather than angry and alienating. Another result of Christ's words remaining in Christians' consciousness is that their petitions reflect Christ's concerns, and thus the Father is fully disposed to assent to them. The Father is also glorified when Christians bear evangelistic fruit because of their union with the Son. Jesus passes on his Father's love to his disciples, and urges them to remain in his love and not walk away from it. If they remain in Christ's love, Christians will experience his joy, even to overflowing.

Though a command to remain in Christ's love may sound strange, it is necessary because of human fear of love, even Christ's love. One has to be vulnerable to accept love, and therefore must trust the lover. Unless we remember Christ's love for us personally, it is hard to trust even Christ enough to surrender to him all control over our own lives, which is necessary to remain in his love. We have to surrender control of our lives to Jesus, for the prerequisite he sets for abiding in his love is keeping his commandments, just as he abided in his Father's love by keeping his commandments (Jn 15:10). The Johannine tradition constantly links love of God and Christ with obedience to their commands. Love in John is not a mere emotion or warm feeling, but a demanding reality that is demonstrated by obedience and by laying down one's life for the other: "Greater love has no man than this, that a man lay down his life for his friends. You are my friends, if you do what I command you" (John 15:13-14). Love is therefore primarily related to one's will, choices and actions. God demonstrated his love by sending his Son: "For God so loved the world that he gave his only Son, that whoever believes in him should not perish but have eternal life" (Jn 3:16). Jesus demonstrated his love for his disciples by washing their feet ("having loved his own who were in the world, he loved them to the end," Jn 13:1), and for his Father by rising in obedience to go to his death ("but I do as the Father has commanded me, so that the world may know that I love the Father. Rise, let us go hence," Jn 14:31). We demonstrate our love for Jesus by obeying him: "If you love me, you will keep my commandments" (Jn 14:15; cf. 14:23, "If a man loves me, he will keep my word"; 15:10, "If you keep my commandments, you will abide in my love, just as I have kept my Father's commandments and abide in his love"; and 21:15, "Simon, son of John, do you love me more than these? He said to him, 'Yes, Lord; you know that I love you.' He said to him, 'Feed my lambs'").

The First Letter of John provides several important supplements to the Gospel's instructions about how to abide in Christ.[74] "By this we may be sure that we are in him: he who says he abides in him ought to walk in the same way in which he walked" (1 Jn 2:5b-6). Abiding in Christ requires imitation of Christ, living and acting the way he did in his earthly life. Union with Christ has ethical implications that rule out any kind of antinomian mysticism. Our ethical behavior is a test of how genuine our union with Christ is and of whether we continue to abide in him.

Abiding in Christ also means remaining in the Christian community: "if they had been of us, they would have continued with us; but they went out, that it might be plain that they all are not of us" (1 Jn 2:19). Remaining in Christ demands perseverance in the close union with him and with all others who are "in him." A frequent Johannine expression for this union is love for one's brothers (and sisters). People cannot love God without also loving their brothers and sisters in Christ:

> Beloved, let us love one another; for love is of God, and he who loves is born of God and knows God. He who does not love does not know God, for God is love.... Beloved, if God so loved us, we also ought to love one another. No man has ever seen God; if we love one another, God abides in us and his love is perfected in us (1 Jn 4:7-8, 11-12).

An important sign of love for the community is remaining in the community. Those who leave the community do not demonstrate love for their brothers and sisters in the community. Thus, 1 John adds a "sectarian" dimension to abiding in Christ and in God. Fidelity to Christ includes fidelity to his Church.

Another test of abiding in Christ is fidelity to the original

[74]See S. Smalley, *1,2,3, John* (Word Biblical Commentary 51; Waco: Word Books, 1984) esp. pp xxix-xxxii on links between 1 John and the farewell discourse in John 14-17; R. E. Brown, *The Epistles of John* (AB 30; Garden City: Doubleday, 1982) esp. p 136 bibliography on "abiding, remaining"; cf. Johnson, *Writings NT*, 501-11 on 1,2,3 John as a three-letter packet from the elder.

doctrine of the community. Christians can trust their inner anointing by the Spirit to discern and reject false teaching incompatible with that original teaching.

> No one who denies the Son has the Father. He who confesses the Son has the Father also. Let what you heard from the beginning abide in you. If what you heard from the beginning abides in you, then you will abide in the Son and in the Father. And this is what he has promised us, eternal life.
>
> I write this to you about those who would deceive you; but the anointing which you received from him abides in you, and you have no need that any one should teach you; as his anointing teaches you about everything, and is true, and is no lie, just as it has taught you, remain in him (1 Jn 2:23-27).

At first appearance there is a tension between the concepts of fidelity to the community's original doctrine and of independence from teachers because of one's interior anointing. Some scholars have suggested that this tension may have led to the eventual demise of the Johannine forms of Christian community.[75] Overstress on inner spiritual anointing as a source of truth and defense against false teachers can break down the authority not only of false teachers but of the community's own teachers and doctrines.

The original teaching which Johannine Christians "heard from the beginning" is that no one can abide in Christ without confessing him as Son of the Father. The teaching "from the beginning" probably includes the Gospel's teaching. The author of 1 John is insisting that one cannot know God truly, i.e., as Father, without confessing the Son of God. Therefore one cannot abide in the Father either, without confessing the Son. According to this passage, not only Jews who reject Jesus but Christians with faulty christological beliefs fail to know God in truth. One cannot know or abide in the Father without knowing and abiding in the Son, who is the divine correlative

---

[75]Brown, *Epistles*, 103-15 gives an elaborate scenario.

to the Father and the reason why one names God "the Father." Thus, fidelity to original doctrine is essential for remaining in Christ and in God.

In the light of this insistence on "what you heard from the beginning" (1 Jn 2:24), the further statements about the anointing Christians received from Christ seem to have a specific focus and point. Taken out of context, emphasis on inner anointing could lead to doctrinal anarchy in a community. In this context, the point of the emphasis seems to be limited to protecting the original teaching from false teachers. Christians can detect the falseness of new teachings because they have an inner anointing that does not resonate with such teaching but only with the original doctrine about the Son and the Father. The writer of 1 John appeals to his community's inner anointing to supplement what he is writing them, recalling them to their original confession of the Son. What they originally learned, his reminder in this passage, and their inner anointing from Christ abiding in them combine to protect them against the lies of false teachers.

The threefold tension between original doctrine, inner spiritual anointing and current false teaching can be found in every age. Simply to call people back to an abandoned orthodoxy may be less effective than to appeal also to the inner anointing of the Holy Spirit to whom people have opened their lives, as 1 John 2:27 does. To measure others almost exclusively by orthodox statements and liturgical rules tends to engender negative attitudes and alienating behavior, whereas to emphasize personal repentance, continuing conversion, and reception of the Holy Spirit can combine the desire for orthodoxy with an inner conviction of the truth that does not have to be defensive or offensive to others. Although the latter way may not be as "safe" as exclusive focus on orthodox doctrine, it seems more suited to our real situation as sharing in the fallen conditions we may deplore. Merely to accuse others of false teaching or practice does not address the sin and false emphases in ourselves, in which every human being except Christ and Mary shares.

If like the saints we first admit our own sin and error, accept Jesus' offer of a personal relationship as our savior from our sins and as our Lord whom we obey, and receive his further empowering by the Holy Spirit, we also are converted to true doctrine and moral practice in the community of the Church. But we realize we are forgiven sinners and long to share the good news of our forgiveness with others, whom we invite to the same repentance, relationship with Jesus, empowerment by the Spirit, and true doctrine and moral practice in the Church. Both approaches result in true teaching and practice in the Church, but the way to that result differs markedly between them. The militant approach that mainly judges others' orthodoxy fails to address the personal need for repentance and conversion to Jesus Christ that all people share, and so it tends to divide humanity into insiders and outsiders, right and wrong, good and bad, thus opening doors to self righteousness, legalistic judgmentalism, and alienation. The approach of the saints through personal conversion and empowerment by the Holy Spirit leads to identification with other sinners and evangelistic zeal that is gentle and respectful of others despite their weaknesses and falsehoods. The inner conviction and peace that comes from total submission to God's will and the grace of the indwelling Holy Spirit leads to sharing one's faith and leading others to true doctrine and practice with a quiet and grateful confidence and therefore without harshness and condemnation. That same peaceful inner conviction or anointing by the Spirit enables one quietly to discern and reject false teaching.

The command in 1 John to remain in Jesus adds a sense of perseverance to the meaning of abiding in Jesus: "And now, little children, abide in him, so that when he appears we may have confidence and not shrink from him in shame at his coming" (1 Jn 2:28). Abiding in Jesus involves a choice to remain with him and under his influence, and not to go off on one's own. Those who wander away from Jesus and do not persevere in their union with him will be alienated from him and ashamed and afraid to face him when he comes as judge.

Another result of abiding in Jesus which the letter mentions is freedom from sin. "You know that he appeared to take away sins, and in him there is no sin. No one who abides in him sins..." (1 Jn 3:5-6). 1 John divides humans into those who are in Christ and those who are of the devil: "He who does right is righteous, as he [Christ] is righteous. He who commits sin is of the devil; for the devil has sinned from the beginning. The reason the Son of God appeared was to destroy the works of the devil" (1 Jn 3:7b-8). A sign and result of abiding in Jesus is preservation from sin, which the Son of God came to earth to overcome. Although this preservation from sin and the converse judgment against those who do sin have the appearance of absolute marks of whether or not one is abiding in Christ, the letter relativizes them later when it refers to intercession for a brother or sister who sins (1 Jn 5:16). To understand what the Gospel farewell address means about abiding in Christ, it is enough to see sinlessness as its *normal* result.

The First Letter of John adds further signs of abiding in Jesus: keeping God's commandments, believing in the name of his Son, loving one another, and having the Holy Spirit:

> And this is his commandment, that we should believe in the name of his Son Jesus and love one another, just as he has commanded us. All who keep his commandments abide in him, and he in them. And by this we know that he abides in us, by the Spirit which he has given us. (1 Jn 3:23-24)

The notions of obeying God's commandments and loving one another have been major themes related to abiding in God and Christ. We have also seen that believing in the name of God's Son is an aspect of abiding in him (1 Jn 2:23-24). The new emphasis here is that the Holy Spirit is a sign that God abides in us (1 Jn 3:24).

A later passage repeats this: "By this we know that we abide in him and he in us, because he has given us of his own Spirit" (1 Jn 4:13). For the Holy Spirit to be a sign by which "we know that he abides in us" (3:24), his presence has to be experienced. To say that we know God's presence in us "by the Spirit which he has given us" (3:24) implies that our gift of the Spirit is something we experience directly, for the normal learning process goes from the better known to the less known, as when one knows one has a fever by the experience of body heat that registers on a thermometer. A mere credal statement about an indwelling Spirit will not provide such assurance "that we abide in him and he in us" (3:24). The letter does not elaborate how we know or experience the Spirit which is given to us but seems to presume that knowledge in its implied readers. The writer expected his readers to know immediately what he meant by his reference to the Spirit given to them. For contemporary readers, previous Johannine treatment of the Paraclete's coming and Jesus' peace can fill in some of their gaps about how Christians are expected to have experienced the Spirit. Awareness of the Holy Spirit must surely include inner conviction, revelation, guidance, and peace, as well as power to "do the works that I do; and greater works than these" (Jn 14:12), e.g., healings, prophetic words and insights into hearts like those of Jesus in the Gospel. One is aware of the Spirit because of the observable effects of the Spirit.

The last signs of abiding in God and Christ mentioned in 1 John are mutual love of Christians and abiding in love, as well as the gift of the Spirit and the confession that Jesus is the Son of God already discussed.

> No one has ever seen God; if we love one another, God abides in us and his love is perfected in us.
>
> By this we know that we abide in him and he in us, because he has given us of his own Spirit. And we have seen and testify that the Father has sent his Son as the Savior of the world. Whoever confesses that Jesus is the Son of God, God abides in him, and he in God. So we know and believe the love God has for us. God is love, and he who abides in love abides in God, and God abides in him (1 Jn 4:12-16).

Love is a key mark of God and of union with God. Love of God cannot be divorced from love of one another. Christians who love one another give evidence that they are abiding in God and God in them. Nor can love of God and neighbor be isolated from confession of Jesus as Son of God and from the gift of the Holy Spirit. 1 John interweaves these signs together in this very brief treatment of abiding in God. Although such commingling of topics frustrates some contemporary senses of logical argument, it bears its own kind of wisdom. Love of God and fellow Christians, experience of the Holy Spirit, and confession of Jesus as Son of God are all central facets of Christian life. Doctrinal confession without love of God and neighbor can lead to harsh sectarianism and judgmentalism. Love of God without love of neighbor is an escapist illusion. Love of neighbor without love of God is neither Christian nor religious. Without the Holy Spirit, doctrinal confession, love of God and love of neighbor lack reality, power, depth and permanence, but the inspiration of the Holy Spirit in turn has to be tested both doctrinally and by love of God and neighbor.

Thus the Johannine meaning of abiding in Christ and God encompasses most of the Christian life. The image of the vine and of the branches abiding in the vine unites and expresses all these aspects of Christian living in a single powerful metaphor. "I am the vine, you are the branches. He who abides in me, and I in him, he it is that bears much fruit, for apart from me you can do nothing" (Jn 15:5).

Jesus' commandment of mutual love among his disciples provides the transition in this farewell address between the topic of abiding in Jesus in the vine in 15:1-11 and the topic of the world's hatred for Jesus' disciples in 15:18-25.

> This is my commandment, that you love one another as I have loved you. Greater love has no man than this, that a man lay down his life for his friends.... This I command you, to love one another (Jn 15:12-13, 17).

Jesus has stressed the union between himself and his disciples, and is about to emphasize the world's persecution of the disciples. The link between these topics is union among the disciples. As they must remain united with Jesus, they also need union with each other, for since the world hates Jesus, it will also hate them. As popular wisdom puts it, "Those who do not hang together will hang separately." Persecuted churches cannot afford the luxury of dissent and disagreement in their ranks. Historically, they have always had to present a united front against their common persecutors, which is why churches behind the iron curtain (like the Polish church) were so united in traditional expressions of Catholicism. The scholarly consensus is that the Johannine church likewise faced persecution and expulsion from the synagogues to which its members originally belonged. This helps explain some of the Gospel's "sectarian" emphases on orthodox belief, unity and mutual love among Christians, and "we versus they" mentality. It also helps explain its continuing importance for persecuted sections of the contemporary Church. I would add that the Gospel's "sectarian" emphases have contemporary relevance also for the American and western forms of Catholicism, which have political freedom to practice their religion but face more subtle forms of persecution, ridicule and attacks on their faith from aggressive secularism.

Jesus' farewell message also refers to how he chose his followers and made them his intimate friends.

> You are my friends if you do what I command you. No longer do I call you servants, for the servant does not know what his master is doing; but I have called you friends, for all that I have heard from my Father I have made known to you. You did not choose me, but I chose you and appointed you that you should go and bear fruit and that your fruit should abide; so that whatever you ask the Father in my name, he may give it to you (Jn 15:14-16).

On the one hand Jesus says that to be his friends we must do what he commands us. On the other, he says that we are more than just servants or slaves, for he does not keep us in the dark about his inner counsel the way masters usually withhold their personal concerns from their slaves. In the Fourth Gospel Jesus has straightforwardly disclosed his identity as eternal Son and Word of God, who has revealed his Father's plan to his disciples. There is no "messianic secret" as in Mark.[76] Jesus' openness to his disciples and his relationship of mutual friendship with them provide assurance to them after he is no longer physically among them. So does the fact that Christ has chosen them, not they Christ. Whereas humans can be inconstant in their choices, Christ is faithful. If Christ has chosen us, we can rest assured he will remain faithful to us and not abandon us in our troubles. Because he has chosen us, he promises us certain and lasting success in our work for him. Because we

[76]Johnson, *Writings NT*, 466-500, p 480.

are his chosen ones, we can also ask the Father anything in his name and expect to receive it.

The theme of the world's hatred and its persecution of Jesus' followers has the important function in Jesus' farewell of preparing them for future adversity, which is one of the standard purposes of farewells.

> If the world hates you, know that it has hated me before it hated you. If you were of the world, the world would love its own; but because you are not of the world, but I chose you out of the world, therefore the world hates you. Remember the word that I said to you, "A servant is not greater than his master" [Jn 13:16]. If they persecuted me, they will persecute you; if they kept my word, they will keep yours also. But all this they will do to you on my account, because they do not know him who sent me (Jn 15:18-21).

It is hard to imagine a more apt description of the meaning and experience of religious persecution of Christians than this reflection on the dualistic opposition of the world to Christ's disciples. Those who follow in Christ's ways must expect the same treatment from the world that Christ received. The world rewards its own, as is to be expected. Those whom Christ has called out of the world, to patterns of belief and behavior that are quite different from the world's, cannot expect the world's approval. Christian beliefs in the oneness of God and uniqueness of Jesus as savior and mediator for all humans contradict the religious indifference and relativism of the contemporary world as intensely as it offended some set beliefs of the Jewish world into which the Johannine church was born. Whether Christians find themselves in states that are secularistic, communistic, Moslem, or even decadently "Christian," they will find themselves at odds with "the world" around them. In fact, because of the fallen state of humanity, believers have always found themselves at odds with their environment even in the most Christian of cultures, for the trio of "the world, the flesh and the devil" constitute the three perennial sources of Christians' experience of temptation.[77] The encouraging note

---

[77] See K. Rahner, H. Vorgrimler, *Theological Dictionary* (New York: Herder, 1965) 454, "temptation."

in Jesus' warning is that "all this they will do to you on my account" (Jn 15:21). Since Christians will be suffering on Christ's account, they can expect his protection and help in their trials. They can be proud to be persecuted as Christians (as 1 Peter 4:16 also declares), even though a natural result of any kind of persecution is a sense of shame at being ostracized.

In fact, the speech turns the blame back on the persecutors and away from the Christians whom they condemn.

> If I had not come and spoken to them, they would not have sin; but now they have no excuse for their sin. He who hates me hates my Father also. If I had not done among them the works which no one else did, they would not have sin; but now they have seen and hated both me and my Father. It is to fulfill the word that is written in their law, "They hated me without a cause." But when the Counselor comes, whom I shall send to you from the Father, he will bear witness to me; and you also are witnesses, because you have been with me from the beginning (Jn 15:22-27).

The speech is reassuring believers that those who refuse to believe in Christ stand condemned because they reject both Jesus and his Father. It is explaining how others could see the same signs from Jesus that they did and still not believe. It resolves with Scripture the perplexity caused by the apparently perverse behavior of those who persecute both Christ and Christians: "They hated me without cause" (Pss 35:19 and 69:5 in Jn 15:25). Finally, it reassures Christians that they have the Paraclete who will bear witness to Jesus in them, because they have been with Jesus from the beginning. It thus affirms that the apostolic witness of the first generation to Christ is sound and guided by the Spirit, even though most of their contemporaries rejected him.

It would be a mistake to concentrate today on the sectarian divisiveness in these verses rather than on their reassurance to believers. The historical circumstances that gave birth to these sentiments are not the most important concern for twentieth-century Christians, except as a warning to them not to misapply the condemnations in verses 22-25 to anyone who disagrees with them. The contemporary Church does not need condemnations of unbelievers as much as it needs reassurance for its counter-cultural beliefs. What is said in John 15 for the first generations of Christians also provides reassurance for the contemporary Church. Today also, Christian beliefs can seem odd and out of touch with contemporary reality. Today also, the basic issue is whether one accepts Christ as the eternal and divine Son of God and as the sole mediator for humans to reach God. This claim seems even more outrageous today in view of the billions who do not know Christ and the multiplicity of contemporary religions. The passage reassures contemporary Christians too that the Holy Spirit guarantees their belief in Christ despite its unpopularity with the *Zeitgeist*. The passage calls Christians of all ages, through the power of the Spirit, to be witnesses of Christ to the world that does not know him, and not to be demoralized or to doubt their own belief because of the unbelief of others.

The speech includes specific predictions of persecution, expulsion from the synagogues, and even death as a further warning against falling away.

> I have said all this to you to keep you from falling away. They will put you out of the synagogues; indeed, the hour is coming when whoever kills you will think he is offering service to God. And they will do this because they have not known the Father, nor me. But I have said these things to you, that when their hour comes you may remember that I told you of them (Jn 16:1-4).

Most critics think that by the time the Gospel was written the Johannine Christians had already experienced the expulsion from the synagogues here foretold. The reference to killing might be merely a general warning, although there are early traditions that testify that Saul thought he was serving God when he participated in the killing of Christians (e.g., Acts 22:3-5: "But I am a Jew ... being zealous for God as you all are this day. I persecuted this Way to the death, binding and delivering to prison both men and women...."; cf. Gal 1:13-14, "For you have heard of my former life in Judaism, how I persecuted the church of God violently and tried to destroy it; and I advanced in Judaism beyond many of my own age among my people, so extremely zealous was I for the traditions of my fathers").

This prediction to keep the disciples from falling away in John 16:1-4 was even more necessary than the speech's earlier ones, for the motivation of this persecution was actually religious. The Johannine Christians experienced an opposition between the religious tradition of Judaism in which most of them had been raised and their contemporary religious experience and beliefs. When forced to choose between one's tradition and upbringing and one's contemporary experience and beliefs, one may wonder whether he or she was mistaken earlier or is mistaken now: "If I cannot trust my earlier convictions, how can I trust my current beliefs?" In the Gospel narrative, Jesus' farewell warning and prophecy forestalled such doubt by predicting it. If Jesus foretold that people would think they were actually serving God by putting Christians to death, this foreknowledge could somehow buffer the shock when it occurred to later readers. "But I have said these things to you, that when their hour comes you may remember that I told you of them" (Jn 16:4).

This prophecy of religious persecution in John 16:1-4 leads into Jesus' promise of the Paraclete who will convict the world regarding sin, righteousness, and judgment (Jn 16:8), which I treated above with other Paraclete passages. That promise in turn leads into Jesus' prediction he will be absent for a time, so they will have sorrow before joy, as a woman in labor has her pain turn to rejoicing in the birth of her child (Jn 16:16-21). "So you have sorrow now, but I will see you again and your hearts will rejoice, and no one will take your joy from you" (16:22). Encouragement of followers saddened by the speaker's imminent departure is a standard element of farewell addresses. The reassurance continues with Jesus' exhortation to ask their needs from the Father, and his promise that they will receive what they ask and their joy will be full (16:23-24).

Jesus ends the speech part of his farewell (before his prayer of intercession) with a contrast between the fact that he has previously often spoken to his disciples in figures of speech, but now is speaking plainly (16:25-30). This brings to mind Meeks' observations about the sectarian implications of "in-group" speech.[78] Whereas before even the disciples may have

---

[78] Meeks, "Man from Heaven," *passim.*

felt like outsiders when they heard Jesus' enigmatic speech, they now sense themselves admitted into Jesus' confidence as he speaks plainly to them. Jesus challenges their claim that now they believe in him because he is speaking plainly, predicting that they will be scattered and will abandon him (16:31-32). Finally, he ties together the motifs of peace, coming tribulation in the world, and reassurance that he has overcome the world. "I have said this to you, that in me you may have peace. In the world you have tribulation; but be of good cheer, I have overcome the world" (Jn 16:33). With these final farewell sentiments, Jesus turns to his Father in intercessory prayer for his followers (Jn 17:1).

Jesus' two prayers in John 17 are especially appropriate to the farewell genre, because the first so clearly provides for Jesus' immediate disciples after his death, and the second so plainly relates to the implied readers. The first prayer begins with asking the Father to glorify the Son that the Son may glorify him:

> Father, the hour has come; glorify thy Son that the Son may glorify thee, since thou hast given him power over all flesh, to give eternal life to all whom thou hast given him. And this is eternal life, that they know thee the only true God, and Jesus Christ whom thou hast sent. I glorified thee on earth, having accomplished the work which thou gavest me to do; and now, Father, glorify thou me in thy own presence with the glory which I had with thee before the world was made (Jn 17:1b-5).

"Father, the hour has come" signals the climax of the narrative. The plot had been leading up to the hour of Jesus' glorification since John 2:4, "O woman, what have you to do with me? My hour has not yet come." In John 7:30 Jesus' listeners "sought to arrest him; but no one laid hands on him, because his hour had not yet come." In John 8:20 Jesus taught in the treasury, "but no one arrested him, because his hour had not yet come." When some Greeks came to see Jesus before Passover, Jesus declared, "The hour has come for the Son of man to be glorified.... Now is my soul troubled. And what shall I say, 'Father, save me from this hour'? No, for this

purpose I have come to this hour. Father, glorify thy name"
(Jn 12:23, 27-28). The farewell supper in John 13-17 began
with the narrator's setting the scene in the context of Jesus'
hour: "Now before the feast of the Passover, when Jesus knew
that his hour had come to depart out of this world to the
Father, having loved his own who were in the world, he loved
them to the end" (Jn 13:1). Finally, Jesus begins his farewell
prayer, "Father, the hour has come; glorify thy Son that the
Son may glorify thee...." (Jn 17:1). This prayer completes
the narrative preparation for recounting Jesus' passion as his
glorification in the last chapters of the Gospel.

The following statement from Christ's prayer recalls the
Gospel's prologue: "And now, Father, glorify thou me in thy
own presence with the glory which I had with thee before the
world was made" (Jn 17:5). The reference to Jesus' glory with
the Father "before the world was made" clearly alludes to the
Word's existence with God before creation:

> In the beginning was the Word, and the Word was with
> God, and the Word was God. He was in the beginning with
> God; all things were made through him, and without him
> was not anything made that was made (Jn 1:1-3).

When this Word who was "with God, and ... was God" (Jn
1:1) became human, his glory had to shine through his
humanity and human deeds. "And the Word became flesh and
dwelt among us, full of grace and truth; we have beheld his
glory, glory as of the only Son from the Father" (1:14). "No
one has ever seen God; the only Son, who is in the bosom of
the Father, he has made him known" (1:18). Jesus' prayer
makes it clear that through his death and resurrection Jesus
will return to God and to his full, pristine glory that he had
with God before creation, which had only shown through in
glimpses during his public life and through signs. His reality as
God incarnate becomes fully revealed through his passion and
resurrection. In its present canonical form John's Gospel
exhibits the highest christology possible without being docetic
and compromising the reality of Jesus' humanity.

Although the whole farewell dialogue looks forward to the
Church's situation after the departure of Jesus, the first of

Jesus' two final prayers especially focuses on the situation of
the disciples immediately after the founder leaves them. Jesus
has manifested the Father's name to those whom God gave
him out of the world. Since they believe God has sent him
(Jn 17:6-8), Jesus prays for them especially:

> I am praying for them; I am not praying for the world but
> for those whom thou hast given me, for they are thine; all
> mine are thine, and thine are mine, and I am glorified in
> them. And now I am no more in the world, but they are in
> the world, and I am coming to thee. Holy Father, keep
> them in thy name, which thou hast given me, that they may
> be one, even as we are one. While I was with them, I kept
> them in thy name, which thou hast given me; I have guarded
> them, and none of them is lost but the son of perdition, that
> the scripture might be fulfilled (Jn 17:9-12).

Jesus' prayer is especially concerned with providing after his
departure for those whom God had given to him. Although
Christ's disciples have alienated themselves from the world in
order to follow Jesus, Jesus is now leaving them in the world
as he returns to the Father. In this prayer, therefore, he asks
the Father to protect and preserve them after he is gone, just
as he himself had protected and kept them while he was with
them. He will not leave them orphans, as he had promised
earlier in the speech (Jn 14:18). He gives them his own Father
to be their Father (v 11).

A major temptation in the Johannine contrast between the
world and the followers of Christ is flight from the world.
Jesus' prayer meets this temptation head on:

> But now I am coming to thee; and these things I speak in
> the world, that they may have my joy fulfilled in themselves.
> I have given them thy word; and the world has hated them
> because they are not of the world, even as I am not of the
> world. I do not pray that thou shouldst take them out of the
> world, but that thou shouldst keep them from the evil one.
> They are not of the world, even as I am not of the world.
> Sanctify them in the truth; thy word is truth. As thou didst
> send me into the world, so I have sent them into the world.

> And for their sake I consecrate myself, that they also may
> be consecrated in truth (Jn 17:13-19).

Jesus does not want his disciples to flee the world itself, but
only be protected from "the evil one" (probably an echo of the
Lord's prayer).[79] As the Father sent Jesus into the world, so he
now sends his disciples into the world (v 18). The Father is to
make them holy by his word of truth (v 17), as Jesus consecrates himself [the same Greek word as for "make holy"] on
their behalf. The consecration of Jesus (who is already the
"Holy One of God" [Jn 6:69]) on their behalf implies that his
coming passion has sacrificial connotations.[80] To equip his
followers after his death for the mission on which he is sending
them, Jesus consecrates himself for them and asks the Father
to consecrate them in the truth with which they are to meet the
world. Though these words apply directly to the disciples at
Jesus' farewell, they are naturally applicable to all later
Christians as well. We too are in this world but not of it. Jesus
also sends us sanctified with God's word of truth to meet the
world.

Jesus' second prayer in verses 20-26 refers to the recipients
of the original disciples' message and to later generations of
Christianity, the implied readers: "I do not pray for these only,
but also for those who believe in me through their word"
(Jn 17:20). This is as direct a reference to the implied readers
as one is apt to find in any narrative. The implied readers are
not the original disciples for whom Jesus prayed in verses
6-19, and whose word was instrumental in the belief of others.
The implied readers are "those who believe in me through
their word" (Jn 17:20), the future generations whose faith de-
pends on the witness of the first followers of Jesus, and in this
case, especially on the witness of the disciple whom Jesus
loved. Jesus looks beyond his disciples in the narrative to the
future believers whom they will evangelize. This looking into
the future is common in biblical farewell addresses, as clas-
sically exemplified in Jacob's farewell, which prophesies even

---

[79]Lindars, *John,* 527.
[80]Ibid., 528-29.

the readers' future: "The scepter shall not depart from Judah, nor the ruler's staff from between his feet, until he comes to whom it belongs, and to him shall be the obedience of the peoples" (Gen 49:10). The readers of John are clearly envisaged as recipients of the word of the disciples (including especially the beloved disciple) at Jesus' farewell and as belonging to that tradition. Jesus prays explicitly for them also.

It seems most unlikely that whoever wrote these words in their present form and setting was consciously thinking of centuries of future readers, although nothing in the text limits its application to only the implied readers who were in the writer's consciousness. Jesus' prayer for all future believers, including the Gospel's implied readers, focuses especially on their unity, which must have been of special concern as the author envisaged the implied readers' situation.

> I do not pray for these only, but also for those who believe in me through their word, that they may all be one; even as thou, Father, art in me, and I in thee, that they also may be in us, so that the world may believe that thou hast sent me. The glory which thou hast given me I have given to them, that they may be one even as we are one, I in them and thou in me, that they may become perfectly one, so that the world may know that thou hast sent me and hast loved them even as thou hast loved me (Jn 17:20-23).

The prayer speaks of the unity of the implied Christian readers as a sign by which the unbelieving world can believe that the Father sent Christ. To achieve such unity, Christ gives them "the glory which thou hast given me" (v 22) as revealer of the Father.[81] As Christ reveals the Father through his unity with the Father, future believers are to bear witness to the unity between Father and Son by their own unity. Conversely, their unity will witness to the world that God loves them as he loves Christ, for such unity among fallen humans is not possible without the loving help of God, who saves them from their self-centeredness.

---

[81] Ibid., 530.

That God loves those future Christians who are the Gospel's implied readers gives them a share in the special claim for the beloved disciple that he was the one "whom Jesus loved" (Jn 13:23).

> Father, I desire that they also, whom thou hast given me, may be with me where I am, to behold my glory which thou hast given me in thy love for me before the foundation of the world. O righteous Father, the world has not known me, but I have known thee; and these know that thou hast sent me. I have made known to them thy name, and I will make it known, that the love with which thou hast loved me may be in them, and I in them (Jn 17:24-26).

Jesus' prayer makes several verbal connections between the disciple whom Jesus loved and "those who believe in me through their word," the implied readers. Jesus prays that the many [plural] future disciples become perfectly one [as the single beloved disciple], "so that the world may know that thou hast sent me [to which the beloved disciple had been a special witness] and hast loved them even as thou hast loved me [and Jesus had loved the beloved disciple]" (Jn 17:23). In other words, Jesus prayed that the future disciples also become beloved disciples, so completely one that they become "the beloved disciple," the disciple whom the Father (who is one with Jesus) loved. He prayed further that "the love with which thou hast loved me may be in them, and I in them" (17:26), so that they become even more "the disciple whom [the Father and] Jesus loved."[82]

The prayer of Jesus "for those who believe in me through their word" (Jn 17:20) applies to the implied readers the attributes of "the disciple whom Jesus loved." Since Jesus requests for the implied readers the same blessings enjoyed by the beloved disciple in the narrative, the plot guides the readers to fill in its gaps about him at least partially by identifying themselves with him. The implied readers are to be like the disciple whom Jesus loved, and to identify themselves with

[82]Cf. Byrne, "Beloved Disciple," 94.

that beloved disciple in the narrative. Thus they are called to enjoy special intimacy and communion with Christ on his breast (Jn 13:23), to have Jesus' mother (both Mary and the Church) as their mother (19:26-27), to bear witness that blood and water flowed from the side of the crucified Son of God (19:35), to be "first" to believe in his resurrection (20:8), to recognize the risen Christ in his marvelous deeds among his disciples (21:7), and to remain and bear witness to the gospel until Jesus' coming (21:22-24). Such typological identification by the implied readers with the beloved disciple in no way distracts from his historical reality and importance to them as source of the gospel tradition on which their community is based (21:24) but actually enhances his historical importance to them.[83] Jesus' intercessory prayer for the first and later generations of believers after his death brings the great themes of the farewell in John 13-17 to a climax. It relates many of its promises to the implied readers and sets the stage for the passion and resurrection narrative to follow.

[83]See Hawkin, "Function," 140-42, esp. the bibiographical n 25, and 144-46; Brown, *Community,* 31-34, 83 n 157; Schnackenburg, *St. John,* 3.376-80, 382, 386, who emphasizes the disciple as witness to the passion and as the Gospel's guarantor.

Conclusion

It should now be evident that farewell addresses have special impact on relating biblical narratives to implied and even contemporary readers. The special link between farewell addresses and the death of someone loved and revered gave special urgency to his parting words. In the final discourses certain concerns emerged as especially important for later generations. OT and Intertestamental farewell addresses exemplified their uses to show transition to later generations, succession of authority figures, and blessings for future readers. Paul's farewell in Acts 20 underlined the importance of Church authority, the preservation and handing on of genuine apostolic traditions, and good example of Church leaders. Jesus' farewell at the last supper in Luke 22 demonstrated the special importance of the Eucharist and of Church authority as service, as well as illustrating the succession of the twelve apostles with Peter as their head to Jesus' leadership over the restored Israel, the Church. John 13-17 described Jesus' rich legacy to his Church, such as his footwashing example of leadership as service, his gift of the Holy Spirit as Paraclete, abiding in Jesus as branches in the Vine, the uniqueness and necessity of Jesus' truth in the midst of relativism, and peace amidst even persecution.

The genre of farewell addresses explicitly relates the time of the narrative in which they appear to the time after the narrative's ending. They thus have special relevance to later generations for whom the narrative is intended, who are sometimes even mentioned: "I do not pray for these only, but also for those who believe in me through their word" (Jn 17:20). Because of this, the farewell discourses seem more readily susceptible to hermeneutical application to lives of the readers than other parts of narratives about past events. For example, it is not surprising that the First Letter of John, which applied concerns from John's Gospel to lives of Christians in Johannine communities, is more closely related to the farewell address in John 13-17 than to other parts of the Gospel. Because the genre itself addresses the future of the readers, this treatment of NT farewell discourses has maintained a more consistent focus on discussing the religious issues raised by the texts and applying them to contemporary Christian readers than would most treatments of other parts of the Gospels. The genre lends itself readily to holistic canonical approaches and hermeneutical applications like this one, which concentrated on the final narrative whole in its biblical context even when the address was composed of multiple sources.

The primary focus of NT farewell addresses is the legacy from the past to the present Christian community. They ground the present in the past and emphasize continuity with Jesus, the founder of the community, and Paul, his special apostle to the nations. They locate the present community in relation to Jesus and the apostles, as the bicentennial celebration of the constitution recalls Americans to the purposes for which the United States was founded. Therefore the focus of farewells is more preservative than innovative. For many churches in America which are marked more by innovation and adaptation than by awareness of their biblical and traditional roots, study of these farewell addresses can provide a salutary counterbalance to contemporary trends. They recall the importance of apostolic succession and authority for the preservation of the original gospel message against perversions from the American culture and *Zeitgeist*. They remind us of the sacrificial dimensions of Jesus' self-giving presence in the Eucharist, and how the eucharistic celebrant represents Jesus to the community when saying "This is my body," in his stead. They remind us that church leaders are to wash the feet of the community by the way they exercise their authority. They recall the importance of the Holy Spirit as Paraclete guiding, defending, and consoling Christians in their struggle amidst temptations from the world, the flesh and the devil, and reassure Christians of Jesus' abiding presence with them even in persecution. They encourage Christians in America to maintain a counter-cultural witness of Jesus' values to their environment, and not to allow their identity to be swallowed up in the relativism and secularism that surrounds them.

It is hoped that this study of farewell addresses in the NT has not only shed light on some powerful NT passages, but has helped interpret our present situation as followers of Christ in the light of God's plan. When a difficult contemporary situation like secularistic persecution or confusion among ordinary Christians caused by false theological teaching is placed in the context of prophecies and provisions by Christ or by Paul, it no longer appears meaningless but is seen as subject to the providence of God. Their farewell addresses in the NT show both Jesus and Paul as foreseeing and preparing for false teaching, persecution, and struggles to be Christian in a hostile environment. For such difficulties, their farewell discourses promise the help of the Holy Spirit and the oversight of apostolic authorities. Assuring us that Jesus Christ continues to be present among Christians, who are to abide in his love and truth, the farewell addresses from the NT continue to speak to our own times.

Bibliography

This is a very brief list of titles by which readers can pursue some of the topics which this book discusses. Among these I include some of my own publications to give further argument and selected bibliography for positions in this book. As immediate background for the New Testament farewell addresses in Acts 20, Luke 22 and John 13-17, I recommend reading other examples of testaments within the canonical (including deuterocanonical) writings available in Bibles: 1 Kg 2:1-10 (David), 1 Sam 12:1-25 (Samuel), 1 Macc 2:49-70 (Mattathias), Joshua 23-24, 1 Chr 28-29 (David), Tob 14:3-11 (Tobit), Gen 49 (Jacob), Deut 31-34 (Moses). For some non-biblical examples, see Charlesworth below.

Brown, Raymond E., *The Gospel and Epistles of John: A Concise Commentary* (Collegeville: Liturgical, 1988).

Byrne, Brendan, "The Faith of the Beloved Disciple and the Community in John 20," *Journal for the Study of the New Testament* 23 (1985) 83-97. He views the beloved disciple as a "point of insertion" for later generations into the pivotal events of the Gospel.

Charlesworth, James H., ed. *The Old Testament Pseudepigrapha* Vol. 1: *Apocalyptic Literature and Testaments* Garden City: Doubleday, 1983. Note esp. the texts of non-biblical testaments like Testaments of the Twelve Patriarchs and the Testament of Moses, with introductions.

Collins, John J., "Testaments," *Jewish Writings of the Second Temple Period* ed. M. E. Stone (CRINT 2.2; Philadelphia: Fortress, 1984) 325-55.

Johnson, Luke Timothy., *The Writings of the New Testament: An Interpretation* (Philadelphia: Fortress, 1986): "Luke-Acts," 197-240; "The Gospel of John," 469-500;

"1, 2, and 3 John," 501-11. An excellent introduction in a single volume to the writings to which these farewell addresses belong.

Kolenkow, Anita B., "The Literary Genre 'Testament,'" *Early Judaism and Its Modern Interpreters*, ed. R. A. Kraft and G. W. E. Nickelsburg (Philadelphia/Atlanta: Fortress/Scholars, 1986) 259-267, bibliography 279-285.

Kurz, William S., "Luke 22:14-38 and Greco-Roman and Biblical Farewell Addresses," *Journal of Biblical Literature* 104 (1985) 251-68.

_____, "Narrative Approaches to Luke-Acts," *Biblica* 68 (1987) 195-220.

_____, "The Beloved Disciple and Implied Readers," *Biblical Theology Bulletin* 19/3 (July 1989) 100-07.

Maddox, R., *The Purpose of Luke-Acts* (FRLANT 126; Göttingen: Vandenhoeck & Ruprecht, 1982) 158-79 (ch 6, "The Special Affinities of Luke and John").

Neyrey, Jerome, *The Passion According to Luke: A Redaction Study of Luke's Soteriology* (Theological Inquiries; New York: Paulist, 1985) 5-48 treats Luke 22:14-38 as a farewell speech.

von Speyr, Adrienne, *The Farewell Discourses: Meditations on John 13-17* (San Francisco: Ignatius, 1987) translated by E. A. Nelson: a Catholic mystic applies her understanding of the farewell in John to contemporary life.

Author Index

Subject Index

Scripture References

Old Testament

Genesis

1-3	38, 39
1:31	38
2:24-25	39
3	38
3:5	38
3:7	39
3:7-12	62
3:11	39
3:12-13	39
3:16-17a	39
3:23-24;	
4:5-10	39
4-11	38
34:25-30	28
49	21, 24, 25, 27, 31
49:1	28
49:3-4	28
49:5-7	31
49:8-10	28, 67
49:8-12	24, 31
49:10	24, 118
49:13-21	28
49:22-26	28
49:27	28
49:29-32	28
49:33	29

Exodus

32:26-29	28

Deuteronomy

31	29
31; 32:44-	
33:1; 34	29
31-33	21
31-34	29, 31
31:2	29
31:2-6, 7-8, 10-13, 26-29	29
31:6	29
31:7	29
31:8	29
31:9-13	29
31:14, 16-21	29
31:14-15	29
31:14-23	29
31:14-17, 19, 21-23	30
31:16-17	30
31:19	30
31:21	30
31:24-29	30
31:30	30
32	29
32-33	29
32:1-43	30
32:44	30
32:46-47	30
32:48-52	31
33	21, 29, 31
33:2-5	31
33:6	28
33:7	31
33:8-11	31
33:13-17	28
33:16	31
33:26-29	31
34	31
34:1-8	31
34:9	31
34:10-12	31

Joshua

23-24	31

Judges

5:15-16	28
11	28

1 Samuel

2:12-17, 22-25; 3:11-14	49
12	31
12:3-5	48

2 Samuel

11	14

1 Kings

2:1-9	16
2:1-10	31
2:8-9	16

Psalms

35:19; 69:5	111
41:9	62
80:8-16	94

Isaiah

5:1b-5	94
11:1-9	28
21:6	44
44:7	87
53:12	68

Jeremiah

2:21	94
6:17	44

Other Ancient Texts Alphabetically

1 Clement

44	65

Jos. *Ant.*

4.8.45-49, 309-31	29
12.6.3, 279-81	25,26
12.6.3, 279-84	25, 31
12.6.3, 280	26
12.6.3, 282	27
12.6.3, 283	27
12.6.3, 284-85	27

Jub.

21	28
22:10-30	32
35:18-20	27, 28
36	28

Phaedo

115c	69
115c-e	69
115e-116a	69

Ps.-Philo, *Bib. Ant.*	19, 29
T. 12 Patr.	28, 31
T. Mos.	29, 31